the impatient beader
gets inspired!!

by MARGOT POTTER

NORTH LIGHT BOOKS
CINCINNATI, OHIO
www.artistsnetwork.com

Meet The Impatient Beader

Margot Potter has been designing jewelry for over ten years, and her step-by-step jewelry designs and word stylings can be found in *Simply Beads Magazine*, where she is a regular contributor. Ms. Potter can also be seen gracing the television screen on QVC as a jewelry line spokesperson. She is the author of *The Impatient Beader*. However, she is far more than a mere designer, TV personality and author. She has also been, in alphabetical order, an actress; a backyard chicken keeper; a magna cum laude college graduate; a mom; a poet; a retail proprietress; a thrift store treasure repurposer; a vocalist of the alt rock, swing, blues and country varieties; and a waitress/psychologist.

Margot lives in a 125-year-old Amish school house with her family and an ever-increasing menagerie of animals near Lancaster, Pennsylvania. In addition to her many jobs, she spends a lot of time with the most important person in her life, her awesome daughter Avalon. Having completed the world's sparkliest tiara, she is now at work on the world's largest ball of string…okay…not really…but she is busy packing her bags for an exciting new adventure.

11 10 09 08 07   6   5   4   3   2

Library of Congress Cataloging-in-Publication Data

Potter, Margot.
  The impatient beader gets inspired : a crafty chick's guide to fabulous design / Margot Potter.
    p. cm.
  Includes index.
  ISBN-13: 978-1-58180-854-4 (alk. paper)
  ISBN-10: 1-58180-854-2 (alk. paper)
  1. Beadwork. 2. Jewelry making. I. Title.
  TT860.P683 2006
  745.594'2--dc22
                              2006002633

Distributed in Canada by Fraser Direct
100 Armstrong Avenue
Georgetown, ON, Canada L7G 5S4
Tel: (905) 877-4411

Distributed in the U.K. and Europe by David & Charles
Brunel House, Newton Abbot, Devon, TQ12 4PU, England
Tel: (+44) 1626 323200, Fax: (+44) 1626 323319
Email: postmaster@davidandcharles.co.uk

Distributed in Australia by Capricorn Link
P.O. Box 704, S. Windsor, NSW 2756 Australia
Tel: (02) 4577-3555

Editor: Jessica Gordon
Cover Designer: Karla Baker
Interior Designer: Stephanie Goodrich
Layout Artist: Kathy Gardner
Production Coordinator: Greg Nock
Photographers: Christine Polomsky, Tim Grondin and Hal Barkan
Stylist: Jan Nickum
Illustrator: Vladimir Alvarez

fw
F+W PUBLICATIONS, INC.

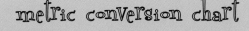

metric conversion chart

TO CONVERT	TO	MULTIPLY BY
Inches	Centimeters	2.54
Centimeters	Inches	0.4
Feet	Centimeters	30.5
Centimeters	Feet	0.03
Yards	Meters	0.9
Meters	Yards	1.1
Sq. Inches	Sq. Centimeters	6.45
Sq. Centimeters	Sq. Inches	0.16
Sq. Feet	Sq. Meters	0.09
Sq. Meters	Sq. Feet	10.8
Sq. Yards	Sq. Meters	0.8
Sq. Meters	Sq. Yards	1.2
Pounds	Kilograms	0.45
Kilograms	Pounds	2.2
Ounces	Grams	28.3
Grams	Ounces	0.035

For my daughter Avalon, with love

"Twenty years from now, you will be more disappointed by the things you didn't do than by the ones you did. Sail away from the safe harbor. Catch the trade winds in your sails. Explore. Dream. Discover."

—Mark Twain

take a bow

To Drew, I love you. To my mom…thank you for being the first person to open my eyes to the inspiration in the world around me. To Linda Potter, thank you for your immense amounts of patience, moral support and babysitting. To the world's greatest editor, Ms. Jessica Gordon, next time let's put you in the starting position! To Christine Polomsky, without you to laugh at my stupid jokes, a photo shoot would last an eternity…and your photos are pretty bitchin' too! To Tricia Waddell and Christine Doyle, even though you give me funny looks sometimes, I am glad you also gave me such tremendous opportunities! To Stephanie, thanks for your inspirational design. To the F+W team…no one compares! To Vlad, you are a cartoon master! To Miss Kim Paquette, thanks for the sparklies! To Wyatt and Fernando, thanks for your deeply appreciated support! To Miss Yvette, thanks for giving me a push, chica! To all of the wonderful companies that provided me with such amazing product, thank you for giving me endless creative inspiration and for helping me to inspire my readers! To anyone whom I have neglected, don't neglect to let me know.

"So shines a good deed in a weary world."

—William Shakespeare via Willie Wonka

the goods

Wild Women 42

All Hail the Bead Queen 22

Get Inspired
find your inner art girl

IF YOU ARE BUYING THIS BOOK, I'M WILLING TO BET YOU WERE A CREATIVE KID. Your biggest joy was a fresh box of 64 Crayola crayons, you made fabulous mud pies with elaborate stone icing, you collected random bits of cool stuff to keep on a shelf by your bed, you made wonderful, fantastical creatures out of Play-Doh…need I go on? You didn't care what color things were supposed to be or if the scale was wrong or what the rules were. Heck, you didn't even know there were rules. You created stuff because it was fun and you couldn't help yourself. Then somewhere along the way someone told you that you weren't an "artist," and your creative fire sputtered out.

The "arbiters of artiness" are everywhere, ready to burst your creative bubbles. They will explain to you in great detail that grass is green and flowers do not float in the air or that you must color inside the lines.

I have certainly had experiences that lead me to believe I wasn't arty enough for the art club. It took me years to realize that I did indeed have a unique creative voice that demanded to be heard, and I finally quit my day job and became a freelance designer. Now I play all day with jewelry and craft supplies and get paid to create cool stuff. How would you like to rediscover your creative voice and see where it leads you? How would you like to tell the artsy fartsy know-it-alls to kiss off? How would you like to discover the little person inside of you dying to come out and play? Well, this book is designed to help you do just that!

In the pages that follow, you will learn easy ways to pull design inspiration from the world around you to make fabulous jewelry and accessories. You will be introduced to a delightful diversity of fun techniques like jewelry making, découpage, soldering, embroidery, Hot Fix crystal application, polymer clay and more. Every project is fun to make and every technique is easy to master. Every chapter is a celebration of all things arts and craftastic. So, get out a smock and beret and forget the naysayers—you are about to reintroduce yourself to your inner art girl! Hip, Hip Hooray!

skill level guide

The designs in this book are rated for your creative safety. Don't be afraid to move beyond your creative comfort zone—there is no failure beyond the failure to at least give it a whirl…right?!

If you're a **crafty Virgin,** you'll find these simpler projects the easiest.

If you're a **crafty Vixen,** you're ready to step it up a little and try something a bit more challenging.

If you're a **crafty goddess,** well, then you can do anything you want. If you want a challenge, these projects are for you.

living in a
material world

bead queen's accoutrements

Here are the must-have basic supplies and materials you need to begin your journey into the magical kingdom of the bead queen. After all, a queen must have the proper tools to reign supreme. Round these up, then sit upon your beading throne and create your own "sparkletastic" crown jewels!

Let's face it: A crafty chick needs the proper tools. Gather up a few essentials, and you've got the keys to the kingdom, honey.

A **bead board** is a beader's best friend. The multipurpose flocked and channeled board measures your design length, keeps your beads from skipping off into the sunset and allows you to map out your designs before committing them to wire. Go get one, quick, you'll be so glad you did!

A **bead mat** is a fluffy little fabric mat that keeps teensy beads in place while you work and gives you a place to keep your materials organized. Opt for a bead mat when working with tiny beads, larger charms or other items that just don't lend themselves to the bead board. Beads really love to roll away from you at the worst possible moment, and a bead mat helps keep them in check.

Round-nose pliers are jewelry pliers with a round, graduated pointed tip that provide the ideal foundation for all basic wirework. You can loop and wrap your wire and head pins to your heart's delight with these puppies.

Chain-nose pliers have flat, pointed pincers that live to grasp and pull wires. They are essential for wireworking, especially for manipulating head pins. The thinner the nose, the more freedom you have to work in tight spaces.

Flush Cutters are sharp little wire cutters that make your wire cuts clean and easy. Beading wire and metal findings cannot be cut with scissors. The wire will be compromised and your scissors will be shot.

A **crimp tool** is a specialized pair of pliers used to flatten and fold crimps to create a secure clasp-to-wire connection. The crimp tool gives you a professional finish and helps to make your jewelry designs last. I know this tool is a little expensive, but your happiness is worth more than a few dollars, isn't it?

8

from top to bottom: bead mat and bead board (top), round-nose pliers, chain-nose pliers, flush cutters, crimp tool.

WIRE, CHAIN AND FINDINGS

Sure, it sounds naughty, but these foundation jewelry-making materials are really quite nice. You'll use wire, chain or some kind of stringing material for every project. And you'll find that you use findings for every single piece. Amass a variety of each of these things, and pick and choose what you need for each new project.

Beading wire comes in a veritable rainbow of colors and gauges. The best and most secure wire for stringing beads is a cabled multistrand stainless steel wire. This type of wire comes in a variety of diameters (thicknesses) and should fill the hole of your beads to keep designs from wearing down easily. The higher the strand count, the more flexible and stronger the wire. Wires with higher strand counts are a bit more costly, but it is a matter of quality and durability. Read the packaging carefully for recommendations on what wire to select for your project.

Chain is a terrific medium for showcasing charms and dangles. It adds a modern edge to even the sweetest design. There is a vast array of chain out there, from plastic to precious metal. Try a variety of materials to give your work a little sass.

Other stringing materials include memory wire, rubber, leather, suede, stretch strand…the list goes on. Enjoy working with any and all of these items—each one offers a slightly different set of techniques and results. After all, you are a woman of ever-changing moods, are you not?!

Crimp tubes and **clasps** provide the finishing touches on your jewelry designs. These handy little findings can be entirely functional, or they can become part of the design. It's entirely up to you! Crimp tubes and crimp beads are tiny metal findings that are flattened and folded to connect clasps to wire or to create bead stations. They come in different finishes. Clasps come in all varieties, big and small. Pick what works best for each piece you make.

Head pins and **eye pins** are used mainly to create beaded dangles. Head pins have a flat bottom to secure a bead to make a dangle or an earring. They can be coiled or turned and attached to your jewelry designs with pliers. The eye pin has a looped end for when you plan to create connected beaded chains or charms. Both are available in base and precious metal, the latter being more expensive but far easier to manipulate.

Jump Rings are little metal rings that are a necessity for the jewelry artist. Use jump rings to attach dangles to chains or to connect beaded segments and give them flexibility. Jump rings can also be artfully connected to make elaborate chains and chain mail…if you are truly patient and have a lot of time on your hands. Good luck…

from top to bottom right: head pins, crimp tubes, earring findings, jump rings, toggle clasp, chandelier earring components, lanyards and lobster clasp linked to chain, leather cord, wire, silk cord, elastic, link chain.

Swarovski Crystal is the world's best crystal, without question. This leaded crystal refracts light like nothing else, except a finely faceted gemstone. A company obsessed with perfection, Swarovski crystal is a sparkly delight for any designer.

Glass Beads come in every color and shape from many cultures. Czech glass is my personal favorite and comes in many whimsical shapes, colors and sizes. China and India produce some affordable and fun lampwork (hand-blown) glass beads. Venetian glass is extraordinary. Travel the world simply by exploring the wide variety of handmade glass beads available for your beading enjoyment.

Gemstone Beads are flooding the bead market these days and often provide the perfect inspiration to get your creative juices flowing. It is a good idea to educate yourself about dyeing, heat treating and irradiating stones—that way you know what you are getting and what it is truly worth. Consider gemstones a gift of inspiration to you from Mother Earth, with love.

Playful **Plastic Beads** are the perfect choice for whimsical designs. There are several designs in this book that feature funky plastic charms. Vintage Lucite and Bakelite beads have become very collectible, who knew?

Metal Beads also present the designer with a vast wealth of choices. Many of the newer styles are more affordable versions of handcrafted precious metal beads. Metal beads are great for adding texture and complexity to your designs.

Precious Metal Beads, such as sterling silver, gold-filled and gold findings are more expensive than their base metal counterparts, but they really do give your jewelry a high-end appeal. Sometimes it is worth it to splurge and use the better metal beads, especially to accentuate gemstone beads.

baubles, bangles and bright shiny beads

I am like a crow; I just love sparklies, how about you? Beading is the perfect avocation for a collector of shiny objects. There are countless beads from which to choose, and thus the choices can easily become dizzying. Here is a brief introduction to the most popular styles of beads, many of which are featured in this book, to help you narrow the field. This is only the start of your bead journey; rest assured it will be endlessly fascinating.

beads clockwise from top left: plastic beads, dichroic glass beads, gemstone beads, Swarovski crystals, metal beads, glass beads, seed beads and E beads, precious metal beads.

STICKY FINGERS

All crafty chicks must have a collection of glues, resins and adhesive materials in their repertoire, don't ask why, some things cannot be explained! There are simply never enough sticky substances with which to play, so get a collection together and start getting those fingers glooped up! Think of this as an extension of the paste in a jar you loved to play with in kindergarten; just don't get any kooky ideas about eating these glues, ick!

Mod Podge (Sparkle and Gloss) is the quintessential découpage medium. The name of this particular brand is an abbreviation for "modern découpage." This wonderful stuff was invented by a woman who needed the perfect substance with which to create her découpage masterpieces. And I just love saying the name! Add a subtle touch of glitter with Sparkle Podge.

G-S Hypo Cement is a jeweler's glue with a nifty metal tip that allows you to zero in on knots and slip glue into tight spaces. It has a zillion uses for jewelry designers.

Liquid Resin can be used to add dimension to fabric and paper designs. It is a favorite among the altered arts crowd.

Instant Grrrip Craft Cement works well when you need to tack something into place before sewing or découpaging over it. It works fast, and best of all, has no offensive odor. This is the good stuff.

Clear Resin Stickers come in a wide variety of shapes and sizes and are more fun than a barrel of monkeys. Originally intended for scrapbooking, they are terrific for multimedia jewelry designs. I just can't get enough of these things!

CRAFTY GIRL'S BAG O' TRICKS

If you wander the aisles of a big box craft store, you know it can be total sensory overload. So many crafts, so little time! Here is my list of items you need to complete the projects in this book. Think of this as your materials list for Jewelry and Accessories Crafting 101.

A **Soldering Iron** used with lead-free solder and copper tape to make fun pendants and charms. A **Pasta Machine** to condition polymer clay. **Embroidery** and **Sharp Sewing Needles** for embroidering and sewing on beads, respectively. **Electric Bead Reamer** for smoothing the edges and expanding the drilled holes in your beads. A **Hot Fix Applicator** to use with Swarovski Hot Fix Crystals to sparkle up your wardrobe! A **Craft Knife** for precision-cutting paper and other things. **Gum Arabic** and **Pearl Ex Pigments** to mix together to make a paint you can thin to your desired color intensity. **Permanent Markers** in a nice variety of colors for writing on fabric or to use with rubber stamps on fabric. **Découpage Sheets**, so those of you who do not long to rummage through old magazines and books can still découpage and make altered art with the best of them.

from top left to bottom: pigment powders, clear resin stickers, polymer clay, markers, Mod Podge, Aleene's Stop Fraying glue, Instant Grrrip Craft Cement.

from top left: thread and needle, craft knife, solder and flux, Hot Fix Crystal applicator and Hot Fix crystals, bead reamer, assorted clay tools.

desperately seeking inspiration

The method I use to design jewelry has always seemed simple as pie to me, but when I was asked to explain how I worked for a recent TV appearance, I realized that my eclectic aesthetic might be about as clear as mud to someone on the outside. As I began to formulate a concrete way to explain how I approach my work, the seeds of this book were planted. I think this is a very straightforward approach to design for the beginner, and I hope you will too!

When reigniting the creative fire, you may find you need a little artistic jump start. Get a good color wheel, like the one shown, to help with the basics of color and tone, then start examining your world. Look in your closet and see what you have amassed without even thinking twice about it (besides the plethora of shoes!). Are you drawn to vibrant colors, earth tones, cool colors, pastels? This is your personal palette…surprise, surprise!

Pull out a favorite printed item and look closely at the colors and patterns. Try to decipher what makes this a favorite. Now, can you translate that into a design?

Take a field trip to an art museum to spark all sorts of creative energy. Look at paintings and sculptures and even artifacts to get ideas about color, texture and shape.

Mary, Mary how does your garden grow? Take a walk outside and look for unexpected color combinations. Go for a romp in the woods, pick up random bits of nature that capture your eye, take them home and mull them over for new ideas. This should help you define your aesthetic and then from there you can begin to expand your horizons.

I highly recommend taking cues from professional designers who already have an intrinsic understanding of design elements. Advertisements are designed to catch the eye and draw it in, so they are a terrific place to find inspiration. I love textiles, particularly vintage ones, so they often serve as jumping off points for my designs. I like to think of the designing process as a dialogue. What do you love? What sits on your shelves? Can you find texture, color or thematic (motif) elements that you can transform into your own ideas?

The truth is, once you start to tune your eye, you'll see an endless supply of inspiration all around you. It's all a matter of perception.

• color wheel 101

A color wheel is a wonderful tool for any artist because it shows you how to apply color theory in a concrete fashion. As you move the wheel, you'll see how different colors work together. A decent color wheel covers the basics of color theory for you. Displayed on a color wheel you'll find the entire range of the color spectrum divided into color families. Although every color wheel is slightly different, on the one shown, each color family is further divided into numbered values so that, as you choose color combinations, you may choose colors of the same value (intensity or purity of color). For example, if you begin with a red color that has a value of 2, you might choose a green with a value of 2.

As you may remember from science class (or not), color is basically a trick of light; the way light bounces off of or moves through an object creates the perception of color. Light is expressed in waves, so that when you see a rainbow or a prismatic effect, you are seeing light expressed in color as it moves through water, glass or crystal or another clear medium that bends or refracts the light. Since beads are often cut to refract and reflect light, especially translucent glass and crystal beads, playing with bead color is especially entertaining. To use the color wheel for your designs, I recommend having a color wheel with windows to match the beads (or other supplies) you are using in your designs based on specific color values. This way you are always sure to have a perfectly coordinated combination of colors.

start an art journal

A good place to start developing ideas is in an "inspiration journal." Here you can work out ideas on paper before you start your project. Don't worry if you aren't DaVinci, this is just for you, not for public scrutiny. You can take your journal with you when you go select beads and materials if you like; it's a really useful tool to have in your grasp. If you can, try to attach your inspiration item or a photo of it to the page for reference, to give yourself a tangible way to develop your creative process.

BASIC SUPPLIES
artist sketch journal, colored pencils, sketch pencils, good eraser, color wheel.

color crib sheet

PRIMARY COLORS	red, yellow and blue
SECONDARY COLORS	primary + primary: orange, green and purple
TERTIARY COLORS	primary + secondary: chartreuse, fuchsia, turquoise
TINT	color + white
SHADE	color + black
TONE	color + grey
COMPLEMENTARY COLORS	opposites on color wheel
ANALOGOUS COLORS	three to five adjacent colors

If you don't feel you have a knack for color, it's always good to give yourself some guidelines to follow. It is possible to make some pretty awful designs if your colors aren't digging on each other! However, once you understand a bit about color theory, you can push it aside and let your inner artist emerge. Use the color wheel to help learn theory, but trust your own eye to lead you in the right direction. I rarely pay full attention to the rules...but I do know them.

I have two design ideas here to show you what happens in my head when I am formulating an idea for a design. You can be as literal or as figurative as you like with your inspiration items. Sometimes, as with the bottle cap jewelry at right, the inspiration item becomes a part of the design. At other times, as with the Day of the Dead Pin below, the inspiration item gives you an idea for shape and color. As you look through the projects in this book, you'll see that sometimes it's just the idea or the tone of the inspiration item that is translated into the final designed piece.

day of the dead skull pin

My inspiration for this skull pin came from this amazing fabric—I totally freaked out when I found it. I kept it out in the studio and let ideas bubble in my brain. Then it became clear that I simply had to make a sparkly polymer clay skull pin. So I did. At the photo shoot for this book, we all stopped and made our own pins—it was instant arts and crafts class! The fabric gave us a place to start and provided color, texture and design elements...a road map for our own creative expression. It's as easy as that!

crafty chick's bottle caps necklace and earrings

Two seemingly unrelated items came together here. First, I just had to have the mint-condition vintage bottle caps I found online at Outside The Margins (www.outsidethemargins.com). I had seen bottle cap art and jewelry for years and always wanted to make my own…then I found these adorable metal chick charms at Sacred Kitsch Studio and somehow in my twisted mind, they simply had to come together in a big, bold and funktacular necklace. Of course, in my world, there simply must be just a dash of sparkle and voilá, a design is born. I played with the number of caps, how to arrange them, where to put the chicks…the happy colors in the bottle caps…and of course, I am a sucker for a dorky pun. Okay, your turn!

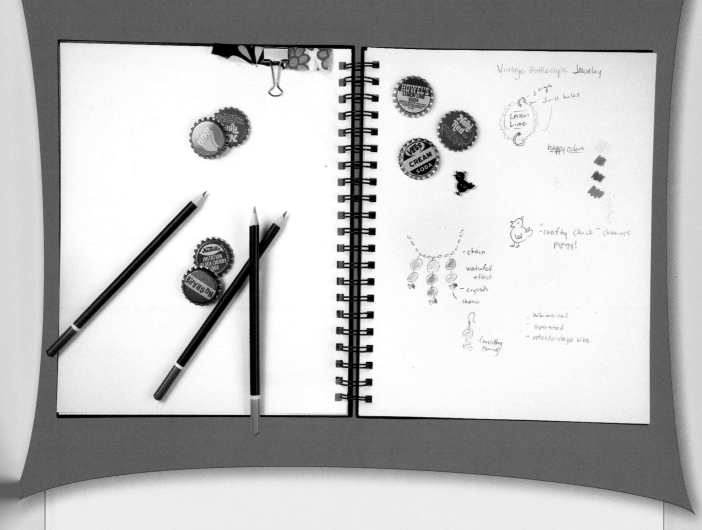

bead basics

Here is a step-by-step tutorial with photos of the basic skills you will need to master for the jewelry-making projects in this book. Practice makes perfect, so don't skip it! Before you know it, you'll be a Bead Master!

• attaching a crimp tube

This is one of the easiest and most secure methods for attaching a clasp to a wire. I highly recommend you use this method to give your jewelry a finished and professional look.

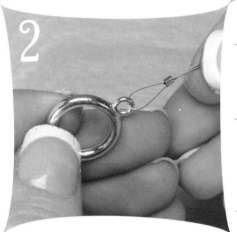

1 slide crimp tube onto wire
Cut a length of wire about 4" (10cm) longer than the finished length of the piece. Thread a crimp tube onto one end of the wire, about 2" (5cm) from the end.

2 slide wire back through crimp tube
Thread the end of the wire through the clasp and back through the crimp tube, allowing a little of the end of the wire to stick through the crimp tube. Slide the crimp tube up on the wire, leaving about 1/8" (3mm) between the clasp and the tube to prevent rapid wear on the wire.

3 flatten crimp tube
Place the crimp tube in the first indentation of the crimp tool. Close the jaws of the crimp tool and mash the crimp tube, smashing it and crimping it flat. There will be an indentation on one side of the crimp tube and the other side will be curved and smooth.

4 fold crimp tube in half
Place the crimped tube vertically into the first slot on the crimp tool with the smooth side facing toward the jaws of the pliers and fold the tube in half.

take it from me

KEEP THE WIRES SEPARATED (UNCROSSED) INSIDE THE TUBE BEFORE YOU CRIMP. YOU WILL HAVE TO HOLD THEM IN PLACE WITH YOUR THUMB AS THEY WILL REALLY, REALLY WANT TO CROSS. YOU WON'T LET THEM, THOUGH, BECAUSE YOU ARE THE MISTRESS OF THE CRIMP TUBE!

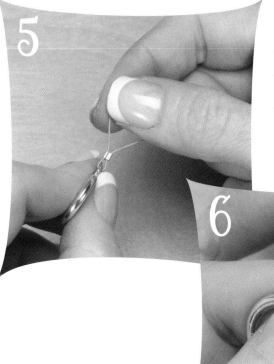

5 make sure connection is secure

After crimping the tube, each wire should be neatly separated by the metal tube, not crossing, as shown.

6 trim end of wire

Use flush cutters to trim the excess tail of the wire, making sure to cut the wire flush against the crimp tube.

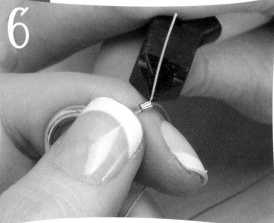

• opening and closing a jump ring

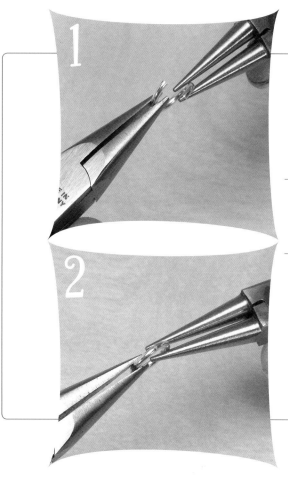

When secured properly, jump rings provide an easy way to attach dangles and charms to your jewelry. Always double-check to be certain the jump ring is completely closed with tension to prevent losing your dangles!

1 open jump ring

Grab the jump ring on either side of the break with round-nose and chain-nose pliers. Move the pliers away from each other laterally to open the jump ring.

2 close jump ring

Use pliers to move the ends of the jump ring back toward each other to close it, again using a lateral movement. Use pressure while moving the ends past each other, then back towards each other until they "click" into place.

• turning a head pin

The turned or looped head pin is an essential skill for making earrings, charms and dangles. Practice makes perfect here—as you master the technique, your loops will continue to improve.

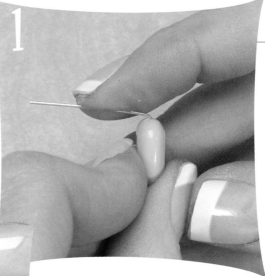

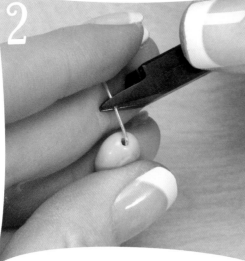

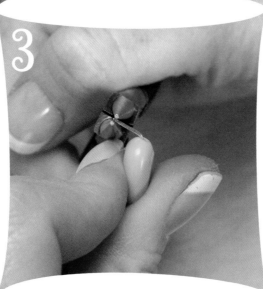

1 bend wire
Slide the bead onto a head pin and bend the remainder of the wire with your fingers at a 90° angle, flush to the top of the bead.

2 cut wire
Use wire cutters to trim the wire about 3/8" (.95cm) above the bead.

3 begin to create loop
Grab the tip of the wire with round-nose pliers.

BEADWORK IS TOUGH ON THE OLD MANICURE. I KEEP MY NAILS SHORT AND THROW ON SOME PRESS-ONS FOR PUBLIC APPEARANCES.

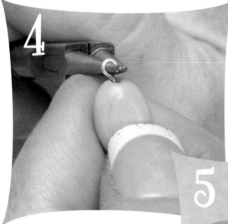

4 create loop

Roll the pliers toward you to create a loop.

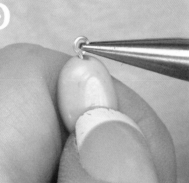

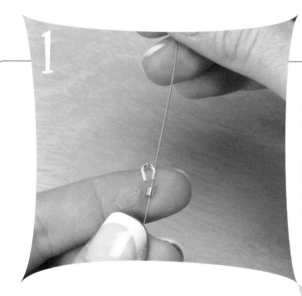

5 tighten loop

Use chain-nose pliers to tighten the loop so that it is fully closed with no gaps.

● using a wire guardian

Ahh, but aren't smart people a boon to jewelry makers? They're always thinking of ways to make life easier and jewelry prettier. Such is the case with the little gem shown here, a wire guardian. Securing wire with a crimp tube is one of the safest and best ways to end and begin most stringing pieces. However, sometimes the bent wire gets stressed out and becomes weak. The wire guardian protects the bent wire and takes some of the stress off of it, making the designs even more secure. You can use wire guardians whenever you use crimps.

1 slide wire through wire guardian

Slide the end of the wire strand through a crimp tube and then through one side of the wire guardian.

2 secure wire in wire guardian

Thread the wire through the other side of the wire guardian and back through the crimp tube. Flatten the crimp tube and fold it in half with your crimp tool.

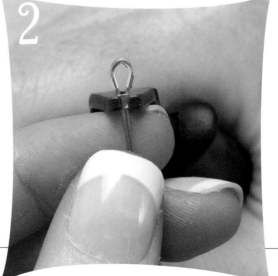

• making a wrapped loop

Wrapping or coiling a head pin is another essential skill for making earrings and dangles. This method creates a secure finish and can also become a decorative aspect of your design.

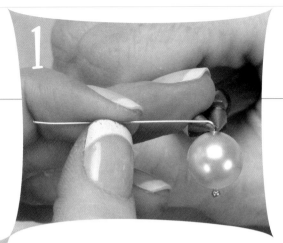

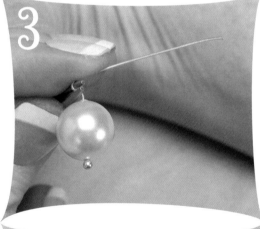

1 bend wire
Slide the bead onto a head pin and grab the wire directly above the bead with round-nose pliers. Bend the wire with your fingers to a 90° angle.

2 grab wire on other side of bend
Position the pliers vertically to the top of the bead to prepare to make the loop.

3 create loop
Use your fingers to bend the wire up and over the nose of the pliers and simultaneously move the pliers toward you to start making a loop. Making a neat, even loop takes practice, so don't worry if it isn't perfect the first few times.

4 prepare to create coil
Continue holding the loop you made with the round-nose pliers and hold the bead between your thumb and middle finger. Begin to push on the tail of the wire with your index finger.

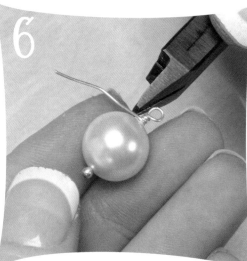

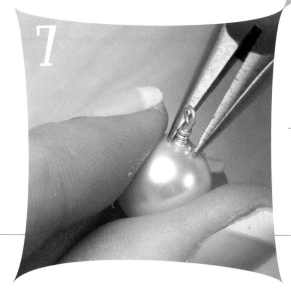

5 create coil

While holding the loop securely with the round-nose pliers, wrap the tail of the wire around the base of the loop. If using a base metal head pin, you may have to use another pair of pliers to help wrap the stiffer metal. Continue to wrap the wire around the base of the loop two to three times until the wrapped wire is flush with the top of the bead. Don't create too much pressure against the top of the bead because glass or gemstone beads can crack or chip.

6 cut excess wire

Cut off the wire tail with flush cutters, again with the flat side facing away from the tail end to make a flush cut.

7 tighten wrap

Tuck the very end of the wire tail into the wrap by tightening it with the chain-nose pliers.

"To cross the river of boredom, one must first hop onto the stone of imagination."
—Anonymous

"For most of history, Anonymous was a woman." —Virginia Woolf

All Hail the Bead Queen

(**designs inspired by beads and pendants**)

A TRUE BEAD QUEEN KNOWS
THAT THE FIRST STEP to mastering her creative kingdom is

the bead shop. There you will discover an entire world of creative inspiration, hiding within one single lovely jasper pendant or handmade masterpiece from
a distant land. The key is to start simply and keep spiraling outward into more complex
designs. Like a creative tornado or a bead goddess…whoosh!

The designs in this chapter are all inspired by focal beads or pendants. By pulling color,
texture and/or motif from a single or multiple beads, designs begin to unfold like the Sunday
newspaper. Be the bead, grasshopper, and all will become clear.

the inside
scoop

the goods

✤ sixty-two 3mm hematite rounds

✤ forty-five 4mm hematite rounds

✤ forty-eight 2mm rice pearls

✤ fourteen 9mm x 8mm cream Swarovski biwa pearls

✤ eight metal flower spacers

✤ eight textured metal spacers

✤ sterling framed stamp or frame your own with a blank frame pendant

✤ two half moon 3-to-1 connectors

✤ SP toggle clasp

✤ four size 2 crimp tubes

✤ three 5mm jump rings

✤ two 19" (48cm) strands of .013" (.33mm) 49-strand wire

the tools

✤ flush cutters ✤ crimp tool ✤ round-nose pliers

✤ chain-nose pliers ✤ two-channel bead board

✤ sandpaper or bead reamer

24

far away places (NECKLACE)

inspiration

vintage postage stamp pendant

When you long to get away from it all, sport this texture-rich double-strand necklace inspired by its focal point, the handcrafted sterling silver postage stamp pendant. Petals from the flowers pictured in the stamp are echoed in the biwa pearls, and the intricate, swirling background is mimicked in the filigree connectors and the textured metal spacer beads. Hematite, white metal and cream pearl beads work perfectly to pull out the stamp's grayscale colors.

1 clip off middle loop of 3-to-1 connector

Lay out the beads on a two-channel bead board in the pattern as written in steps two and three. Before stringing, clip off the middle loop of the 3-to-1 connector with flush cutters. Sand down the metal with sandpaper or a bead reamer to smooth out the metal.

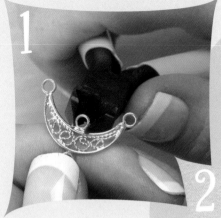

2 attach first strand and string beads

Attach one strand of wire to one of the loops on the connector with a crimp tube (see Bead Basics, page 16). String beads onto the wire in the following pattern: 4mm hematite, rice pearl, two 3mm hematites, rice pearl, two 3mm hematites, rice pearl. Repeat the pattern until the beaded strand is 13" (33cm) long.

3 string on postage stamp charm

Attach a length of wire to the free loop on the 3-to-1 connector with a crimp tube. String the second strand in the following sequence: metal spacer, two 3mm hematites, biwa pearl, two 4mm hematites, flower spacer, two 4mm hematites, biwa pearl, two 3mm hematites, metal spacer, two 3mm hematites, biwa pearl, two 4mm hematites, flower spacer, two 4mm hematites, biwa pearl. Repeat the sequence three times to reach the halfway point, then thread on a metal spacer, two 3mm hematites, a biwa pearl, two 4mm hematites, a flower spacer, then the postage stamp charm and another flower spacer, followed by two 4mm hematites. Begin the pattern again from the biwa pearl and repeat it three times, ending with a metal spacer. Attach the free end of the wire to the second 3-to-1 connector with a crimp tube. Attach this to the circle end of the toggle clasp using a jump ring.

4 attach toggle clasp

Attach the remaining 3-to-1 connector to the bar end of a toggle clasp, making sure to connect the bar end with a chain of two jump rings.

the goods

- large flat brecciated jasper pendant with large center hole
- six approx. 1" (3cm) freeform sunstone beads
- five porcelain faux dzi beads
- eleven 8mm red jasper rondels
- seven 8mm checkerboard faceted smoky quartz round beads
- seven 8mm dyed orange jade coin beads
- fifty-five 4mm faceted carnelian rounds
- textured pewter toggle clasp
- two size 2 crimp tubes
- 5mm SP jump ring
- 2" (5cm) section of 2mm brown leather cording
- three 23" (58cm) strands .015" (.38mm) 19-strand wire

the tools

- two pairs of chain-nose pliers, or one each of chain- and round-nose pliers ✢ flush cutters ✢ mighty crimp tool ✢ bead board

muy caliente (NECKLACE)

inspiration
jasper pendant

When I saw this jasper pendant, I had to snatch it up. Spicy tones of paprika, nutmeg, cinnamon...wait a minute, that was dinner...sorry...ha. I pulled the warm and earthy palette into the beads and the combination of variegated and solid color on one side of the pendant set the asymmetrical tone. Simply add brown linen and chunky sandals and head to the yoga studio in style. Om.

1 crimp wires to clasp

After laying out the design on the bead board, thread all three wires through a number two crimp tube and through the circle end of the toggle clasp and back through the crimp tube. Hold the long strands between your fingers to keep them separated inside the crimp tube. Double crimp. Trim off tails with flush cutters.

2 string first segment of beads

String a smoky quartz and a carnelian onto all three wires. Then begin beading in the following pattern: orange jade, smoky quartz, orange jade.

Patience booster

IT'S ALWAYS A GOOD IDEA WITH ROUGH-CUT GEMSTONES TO SMOOTH THE EDGES WITH YOUR BEAD REAMER. SMOOTHING OUT THE BEAD HOLES HELPS TO KEEP THE WIRE FROM WEARING TOO QUICKLY.

3 separate and bead each strand

Thread three carnelians onto each of the three strands. Continue beading the first half of the necklace in the established pattern (orange jade, smoky quartz, orange jade, three carnelians on each strand). Repeat the pattern three times, ending with an orange jade.

4 bead second half of necklace

Bead the second half of the necklace in the following sequence: freeform sunstone, red jasper rondel, dzi bead, red jasper rondel. Repeat the pattern five times and then string on a freeform sunstone and a red jasper rondel to finish. Crimp wire onto a 5mm jump ring and link the bar end of the toggle to the jump ring.

5 tie on jade pendant

Tie the brecciated stone onto the center of the necklace with a 2" (5cm) length of 2mm leather.

- ⁌ twelve **cereal box charms**
- ⁌ twenty-two **beads from striped bead mix**
- ⁌ twenty-two **metal rondels**
- ⁌ twenty-two **head pins**
- ⁌ **SP lanyard**
- ⁌ **SP lobster clasp**
- ⁌ thirty-six **12mm white jump rings**
- ⁌ thirty-five **SP curved chain links**

crafty Virgin

the tools

⁌ round-nose pliers ⁌ chain-nose pliers ⁌ flush cutters

28

break time (BADGE HOLDER)

inspiration

plastic snack box charms

I don't have the proper constitution to work in an office—my snarky know-it-all attitude makes me far better suited to work from home. I do remember from my brief stint as a temp receptionist that the best part of a day at the office was break time. Remind yourself that break time is near with this totally ridiculous badge holder. You'll be the talk of the water cooler. The vivid colors in the miniature snack boxes complement the funky striped beads, but add other charms as you wish.

1 attach clasp to link chain

Open a jump ring and slide a lobster clasp onto it. Slip the jump ring through the last link in the chain and use round- and chain-nose pliers to close the jump ring (see Bead Basics, page 17).

2 attach cereal box charm to link chain

Slide a cereal box charm onto a jump ring and attach the jump ring to a link in the chain.

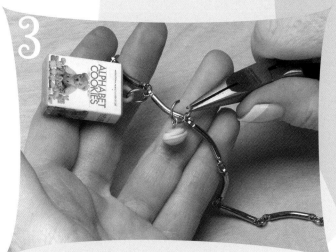

Patience booster

MAKE SURE THAT YOU CAREFULLY CLOSE EACH JUMP RING BY MOVING THE RING FORWARD THEN BACK IN A LATERAL MOTION WITH YOUR PLIERS. IF YOU HAVE THE PROPER TENSION, THE JUMP RING WILL CLICK OR SNAP SHUT. CHECKING IS WORTH THE EXTRA TIME—WHO WANTS TO LOSE A SNACK UNNECESSARILY?

3 attach bead to link chain

Slide a bead (along with a rondel if the bead's hole is too large for the head pin) onto a head pin and turn a loop at the top with round-nose pliers (see Bead Basics, page 18). Trim away excess wire. Slide the dangle onto a jump ring and attach the jump ring to the next link in the chain.

4 attach lanyard to link chain

Attach a jump ring to the end of the chain and attach the jump ring to the lanyard.

the goods

- ❖ crystal chandelier component (rose)
- ❖ three 20mm rose Swarovski stars
- ❖ four 6mm x 8mm lampworked swirled pink, black and white teardrops
- ❖ four 6mm top-drilled black diamond Swarovski bicones
- ❖ four 3mm jet Swarovski rounds
- ❖ eight 6mm top-drilled rose Swarovski bicones
- ❖ twelve crystal AB Czech glass small dagger beads
- ❖ nine 4mm opaque mint green faceted Czech glass rounds
- ❖ Swarovski crystal square channel chain (one forty link section and one forty-five link section)
- ❖ four 20-gauge SP head pins
- ❖ forty-three 7mm SP jump rings
- ❖ two 12mm SP jump rings
- ❖ two SP lanyard components

the tools

❖ round-nose pliers ❖ chain-nose pliers ❖ flush cutters

princess sparkle pants (HIP CHAIN

inspiration
lampwork beads

Inside every girl lives the princess celebrated in this girlie design. My daughter — is very in touch with her inner princess, and she called dibs on this sparkly hip chain the moment she saw it. The lampwork teardrop beads were the source of both the romantic color palette and the delicate design elements. You can opt to wear this connected to your belt loops and draped across your outer thigh or as a pretty necklace (remove one of the lanyards). Make this bit of bling for the part of you that still believes in fairy tales and happy endings.

1 attach chains to lanyards

Link a giant jump ring to each of the lanyards. Then attach each end of both chains to one 7mm jump ring. Attach each 7mm jump ring to the giant jump ring at both ends.

2 make chain dangle

Slide a 6mm black diamond bicone crystal onto a jump ring. Then link that jump ring to a chain of three jump rings, each beaded with an AB crystal dagger. (Hang the daggers on opposing sides as you work up the chain.)

3 attach bead dangles to chain

Beginning at the first chain link, attach beads to the chain every two links in the following pattern: rose bicone; lampwork teardrop with small AB finish jet round; black diamond top-drilled bicone on a jump ring with three daggers on three jump rings; crystal star on a jump ring with three coiled mint green faceted rounds. Repeat the pattern twice. (Note: the stars are embellished with a beaded jump ring, as shown in photo.)

4 attach center circle pendant

Attach the center rose crystal chandelier component to the middle of the bottom chain along with a star dangle.

take it from me

YOU MAY NEED TO ADJUST THE LENGTH TO ACCOMMODATE THE DELIGHTFULLY CURVACIOUS HIPS THAT WILL BE SPORTING THIS DESIGN. JUST WORK YOUR PATTERN OUT FROM THE CENTER POINT AND ADD OR DELETE OUTERMOST DANGLES AS NEEDED.

the goods

- ⊹ handpainted Russian tile bead
- ⊹ three river stones with two holes
- ⊹ three 12mm vermeil filigree open beads
- ⊹ four 20-gauge gold-plated eye pins
- 20-gauge gold-plated head pin
- ⊹ large gold-plated toggle clasp
- ⊹ nine heavy-duty 12mm jump rings

the tools

- ⊹ gold leaf pen ⊹ round-nose pliers
- ⊹ chain-nose pliers ⊹ flush cutters

32

my end is my beginning (BRACELET)

inspiration

handpainted bead and river rocks

The handpainted Celtic-inspired image on the black onyx tile bead inspired – this bracelet centered around the contrast between man-made ornate filigree beads and naturally made tumbled river stones. I added the gold spirals—a shape without start or finish—as a tribute to the eternal mysteries of the universe. As poet T.S. Eliot wrote in his poem "Four Quartets," "In order to make a beginning, there must be an end. The end is where we start from."

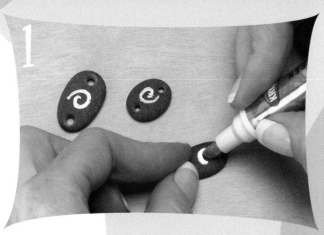

1 draw swirls on stone

Draw a swirl on each river stone with the gold leaf pen.

2 make double-loop beaded segment

Slide a gold vermeil filigree open bead onto an eye pin and turn a loop in the straight end using round-nose pliers (see Bead Basics, page 18). Trim the excess with flush cutters.

3 attach last charm

Link the bar end of the toggle clasp to a double-looped filigree bead with a jump ring. Slide a river stone onto a jump ring and link it to the gold filigree bead. Continue linking river stones and filigree beads together with jump rings until you have used three beads and three stones. Attach the circle end of the toggle to the last river stone with a jump ring. To finish the bracelet, thread a head pin through the Russian painting tile and turn a loop at the top. Link the tile to the jump ring, attaching the circle end of the toggle clasp with another jump ring.

take it from me

YOU MAY OPT TO LEAVE THE LOVELY RIVER STONES UNEMBELLISHED FOR A GREATER CONTRAST BETWEEN THESE AND THE ORNATE FILIGREE BEADS. DO WHAT YOU WANT TO DO—THAT'S HOW YOU REFINE YOUR UNIQUE AESTHETIC.

the goods

- ✤ two freeform-shaped large (1" [3cm] or larger) high-polish apple turquoise pendants
- ✤ six 14mm x 10mm lime turquoise ovals
- ✤ fourteen 8mm x 5mm lime turquoise rice beads
- ✤ twenty 12mm x 8mm turquoise mottle-edge Czech glass rectangle windowpanes
- ✤ one hundred ninety-two turquoise heishi beads
- ✤ fifty 5mm dark green freshwater pearls
- ✤ fifteen 1⅛" (3cm) pewter filigree floral tubes
- ✤ Hill Tribe silver bee pendant
- ✤ two 4-link segments of 12mm x 10mm sterling link chain
- ✤ twelve 20-gauge head pins
- ✤ two SP crimp tubes
- ✤ two wire guardians

the tools

- ✤ round-nose pliers ✤ chain-nose pliers ✤ crimp tool
- ✤ extra long bead board

34

stone cold fox (LARIAT)

inspiration
turquoise beads

Tell me something good…tell me that you love this…lariat! Rich and earthy – shades of green, brown and blue are pulled from the green turquoise pendants into pearls, Czech glass and turquoise heishi beads. Filigree pewter beads provide some contrast and texture and a lovely handcrafted Hill Tribe silver bee flies along for the ride. Purely funkadelic…add hipsters, a gauze shirt, a floppy hat and some chocolate brown boots. Now throw on some Chaka Kahn and get down with your bad self.

1 make beaded dangles

Slide three turquoise ovals and three Czech windowpane beads onto individual head pins. Turn a loop in the head pin wire above each bead using round-nose pliers (see Bead Basics, page 18).

2 attach dangles to chain

Attach two dangles to either side of each of the four links of chain, one oval dangle and one windowpane dangle on each link. Repeat for second chain.

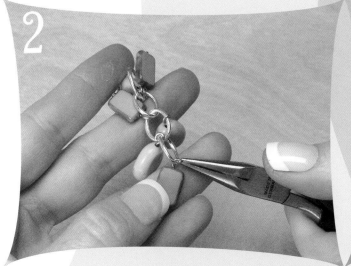

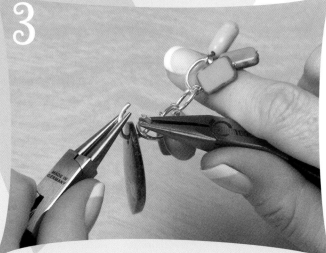

4 slide wire through wire guardian

Slide the end of the wire strand through a crimp tube and then through one side of the wire guardian. Slide wire back through the opposite side of the guardian and crimp tube. Crimp and trim excess wire.

3 add large turquoise bead to dangle

Cut one link from the chain and slide a marquise-shaped apple turquoise bead onto it. Use round-nose and chain-nose pliers to open the link laterally. Close the link to secure the bead. Create the second beaded chain with an oval apple pendant and a Hill Tribe bee on a jump ring at the top of the pendant. Repeat for the other end, omitting bee on second chain.

5 string beads

String the lariat in the following pattern: pearl, 11 heishi beads, three pearls, filigree tube, three pearls, 11 heishi beads, rectangle windowpane, turquoise rice bead, filigree, turquoise rice bead, rectangle windowpane, 11 heishi, three pearls. Repeat the pattern until all of the beads are used, ending with a single pearl. Secure the end of the wire through a crimp tube and wire guardian as before, using your pliers to pull the wire back through the crimp tube, tightening the lariat. Make sure not to make the design too tight, or it will be stiff. Allow some space between the beads to create play. Finish the lariat by attaching the second beaded chain section to the second wire guardian with pliers.

the goods

- handcrafted Russian ceramic pendant ³⁄₈" x ¹⁄₂" (1cm x 1cm)
- eight Mini Craft-t-corks
- fourteen 6mm copper Swarovski crystal rondels
- twelve 4mm chrysolite AB Swarovski bicones
- nine 3mm gunmetal jump rings
- thirty-eight gunmetal eye pins
- gold-tone eye pin
- eight dressmaker's pins
- Pearl Ex pigments in Sparkling Copper and Duo Green-Yellow
- gum arabic
- Sparkle Mod Podge
- fine- and regular-tip black permanent markers

the tools

- flat section of foam/Styrofoam, approx. 2" (5cm) thick
- disposable paintbrushes ÷ paint-mixing plate ÷ round-nose pliers ÷ chain-nose pliers ÷ flush cutters ÷ bead mat

aquatic garden (NECKLACE)

inspiration
handpainted pendant

This beautiful handpainted ceramic pendant from Russia provided me with the raw ingredients for an artsy design. The beads are painted and glazed miniature corks, made to mimic the Klimt-inspired patterns on the pendant. Even though the colors are earthy, the overall feel is very aquatic to me…like a seaweed garden.

1 color cork black

Slide a dressmaker's pin into the bottom of each cork to make a handle. Use a black permanent marker to color each of the mini corks solid black.

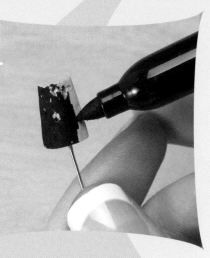

2 paint cork with gum arabic and pigment powder

Dip a small paintbrush into the gum arabic and then into the pigment powder. Swirl the paintbrush around on a smooth surface to blend the gum arabic and the powder. Paint the mixture onto the black corks, painting copper on one end and green on the other. Stick the dressmaker's pins into a foam stand and let them dry for several hours.

3 make markings on cork

Make decorative black markings on each cork that mimic the markings on the handpainted pendant using a fine-tip black permanent marker. When the ink has dried, paint the corks with sparkly découpage medium. Place them back on foam stand to dry.

4 create cork dangle

Cut an eye pin to about $3/8$" (1cm) from tip to end with wire cutters. Use chain-nose pliers to push the eye pin into the top center of the cork to create a dangle.

5 begin to make clasp

Grab the very end of an eye pin with the tip of your pliers and bend the wire back into a loop. At the same time, bend the remainder of the eye pin into a curved shape, using your fingers and the pliers.

6 finish clasp

Bend the eye pin into a U shape and then use your pliers to bend one of the end loops up to create the divot that will accommodate the other side of the clasp.

7 bead and bend eye pin

Thread a bead onto an eye pin. Grab the eye pin on either side of the bead with your fingers and use opposing force to bend it into a curvy S shape.

8 turn beaded eye pin perpendicular

Turn a loop in the other end of the wire by turning the tip of the wire back over itself. In order for this necklace to hang correctly once constructed, the loops of each beaded eye pin must be perpendicular to each other.

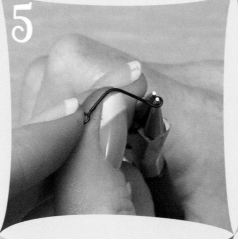

take it from me

YOU CAN USE A COMPLETELY DIFFERENT FOCAL PENDANT HERE AND THE ENTIRE DESIGN WILL CHANGE. SEE WHAT OTHER FINISHES YOU MIGHT RECREATE ON CORK—MAKE GLORIOUS MISTAKES! THAT IS HOW YOU MAKE GLORIOUS ART.

9 link two beaded curved eye pins to clasp

Link one beaded and bent eye pin to the clasp by opening and closing the loop with round-nose and chain-nose pliers. Connect the other end of the curved eye pin to another beaded and bent eye pin, alternating between copper rondels and chrysolite bicones.

10 add cork dangles with jump rings

At every third beaded eye pin, link a cork dangle to the beaded eye pins with a jump ring.

11 create pendant with dangles

Thread a gold-tone eye pin through the handpainted pendant and turn a loop in the straight end with round-nose pliers. Create the dangles that will hang off of the pendant by linking two beaded and bent eye pins together with a cork dangle and then one bent eye pin with a cork dangle. Slide the loop of each dangle onto the eye pin loop at the bottom of the pendant and close the wire loop to secure the dangles.

Vixen

the goods

‡ handpainted Russian Madness pendant

‡ two 20mm x 3mm honeycomb-texture gold-plated metal beads

‡ two 10mm x 8mm frosted-edge crystal AB Czech glass windowpane beads

‡ five 4mm ruby red faceted Czech glass beads

‡ two 12mm cream Swarovski pearls

‡ two 12mm black Swarovski pearls

‡ two 12mm bronze Swarovski pearls

‡ 8mm x 5mm hematite rice bead

‡ 7mm x 5mm hematite faceted bicone

‡ two 5mm x 3mm hematite faceted saucers

‡ sections of jet square channel Swarovski chain in the following lengths: 6-link, 7-link, 8-link, 12-link and two 18-link

‡ ten 3mm gold-plated jump rings

‡ two gold-plated extension chains with teardrops

‡ 8-link section gold-plated medium curb chain

‡ two gunmetal black diamond Swarovski chandelier earrings

‡ 18mm x 12mm gold-plated filigree oval

‡ twelve 20-gauge gold-plated head pins

‡ four 20-gauge gold-plated eye pins

‡ gold-plated magnetic clasp

the tools

‡ round-nose pliers ‡ chain-nose pliers ‡ flush cutters

‡ bead mat

medusa (NECKLACE)

40

A Russian artist handpainted this image from a painting by Gustav Klimt — onto a mother-of-pearl and sterling pendant. Who could resist? The figure is called "Madness"…so the design followed suit. Asymmetrical drops of giant pearls, crystals, filigree components and chain descend randomly from a gunmetal and crystal channel chain. For Siouxsie, Lena and Nina…here i my valentine to the high priestesses of Goth punk…thanks for the dance!

1 arrange chain components

Separate out two 18-link lengths of jet Swarovski channel chain and lay them in a V on your work surface. Arrange the smaller lengths of chain around the two main chains in the following order, from top left to top right: two gold-plated connected extension chains with teardrops at the sixth and tenth channels; seven-link channel chain at the tenth and fourteenth channels; six-link channel chain at the fourteenth and eighteenth links. Starting at the center of the V for the remaining long length of chain, connect an eight-link channel chain to the first and fifth links; the gold curb chain to the fifth link; and the twelve-link channel chain to the fifth and twelfth links.

41

2 make pendant dangle

Thread a gold eye pin through the pendant and make a loop in the opposite end of the eye pin.

take it
from
me

HEY, DON'T FEEL THAT YOU
HAVE TO MAKE THE EXACT
SAME NECKLACE...MIX IT UP
A LITTLE! THE IDEA HERE IS
THAT THE DESIGN BE RANDOM AND
UNSTRUCTURED. I GIVE YOU FULL
PERMISSION TO COLOR OUTSIDE OF
THE LINES!

3 link long chains

Link each of the 18-link square channel chains to the eye pin loops on either side of the pendant.

4 create dangles and link to necklace

Create dangles as shown and connect them to the necklace.

"Life is
either a
daring
adventure
or nothing.
Security is
mostly a
superstition.
It does not
exist in nature."

—Helen Keller

"Hey, babe, take a
walk on the wild side." —Lou Reed

Wild Women

(designs inspired by animals and nature)

EVEN A CITY
GIRL CAN find a lovely weed poking through
the concrete if she makes a little effort. The natural
world is a thing of great beauty, and, it naturally follows, of great
inspiration. Challenge yourself to brave the elements to find some exotic
ideas. Imagine yourself a bold explorer heading off to unmapped territory as you
get inspired by the world around you. Simply apply sunscreen and toss on a jaunty
hat…and get out of the house already. Release the inner wild woman and hear her
roar with delight!

The designs in this chapter are all inspired in some fashion by something from the natural

world. Feathers, fur, flowers…even a farm-fresh breakfast. Ever since I moved to the country

I have rediscovered my love of nature. You may either integrate the inspiration into your

designs or pull ideas from the inspiration item. Either way, you'll feel like a natural woman.

the goods

- ✥ 16mm handpainted rooster bead
- ✥ porcelain handpainted flat circle bead
- ✥ porcelain handpainted large rectangle bead
- ✥ 12mm vermeil milgrain saucer
- ✥ four 2mm x 3mm emerald Czech glass rondels
- ✥ two 6mm marbled red, yellow and white Czech glass rounds
- ✥ ten gold-plated extension chains with ball drop
- ✥ three gold-plated extension lobster chains
- ✥ 6mm gold-plated jump ring
- ✥ four gold-plated eye pins

the tools

- ✥ round-nose pliers ✥ chain-nose pliers
- ✥ flush cutters ✥ bead mat

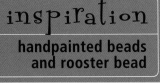

cocky little purse (CHARM)

inspiration
handpainted beads and rooster bead

Cockadoodle do! I have the cutest flock of little chickens, and I highly recommend – them. They provide you with hours of entertainment and tasty egg snacks to boot. All for just a little food, shelter and water…oh, and a goodnight song. Don't ask. This design is inspired by the reverse-painted rooster bead—can you believe someone painted the inside of the bead with a tiny paint-brush? Talk about patience! I'm sure glad they did—this cocky charm looks adorable hanging from a purse strap or belt loop.

1

2

1 link chain to jump ring

Slide a handpainted bead onto a gold eye pin and create a second loop at the bottom. Slide a gold jump ring onto the loop. Remove the lobster clasps from two of the gold-plated extension lobster chains. Link the three chains together and then attach the free end of the linked chains to the jump ring. The clasp will be attached here when worn.

2 connect beaded eye pins

Bead gold eye pins with single beads and combinations of beads as shown. Link the beaded sections together using your pliers to secure the loops closed.

3 finish connectng beaded eye pins

Continue linking beaded eye pins together in the pattern as shown, finishing with the hand-painted rectangle bead. Link the first extension chain to the rectangle with a jump ring.

3

4 attach final gold chain

Attach a total of ten gold extension chains to the jump ring to finish the purse charm. Check back through your work to make sure all of the components are properly secured.

4

the goods

÷ 8mm cream Swarovski pearl

÷ 12mm light green Swarovski pearl

÷ 6mm crystal AB Swarovski rondel

÷ two 9mm x 6mm crystal AB Swarovski teardrops

÷ two 3mm jet Swarovski rounds

÷ two 4mm khaki Swarovski bicones

÷ 20mm jet Swarovski cross

÷ five 20-gauge sterling ball-tipped head pins

÷ five 5mm sterling jump rings

÷ four 8mm jump rings

÷ approx. 18" (46cm) neck-lace-size memory wire

÷ approx. 18" (46cm) 2.5mm rubber tubing

the tools

÷ memory wire cutters ÷ round-nose pliers ÷ chain-nose pliers ÷ flush cutters ÷ scissors ÷ bead mat

how now, grazing cow (CHOKER

inspiration

grazing cows farm fabric

I recently moved to Amish country, and I love it. Everywhere you drive in any direction is farm after farm after farm. My daughter and I joke, "Hey, look, another cow!" This necklace pulls three colors—black, white and green—from the picturesque grazing cows on this barnyard fabric. A rubber tube is fitted with memory wire and simple charms for looking fancy whilst doing the farm chores, à la Eva Gabor in Green Acres.

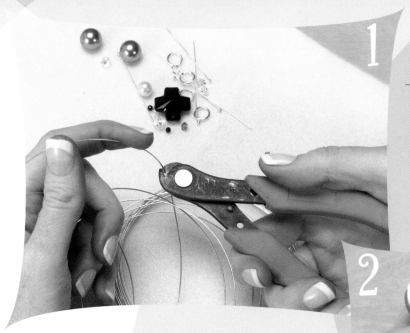

1 cut memory wire to size

Predetermine the length of the memory wire by trying it around your neck to see how it fits comfortably, with some overlap. Cut the wire with memory wire cutters. Turn a loop at one end of the memory wire with round-nose pliers, bending the wire back and over itself to create the loop. (Be patient, this takes a little effort.)

2 cover memory wire with black tubing

Feed the memory wire through the rubber tube. Cut off the tube at the end of the memory wire with scissors. Turn the free end of the memory wire with round-nose pliers.

patience booster

MEMORY WIRE WILL ABSOLUTELY DESTROY NORMAL FLUSH OR WIRE CUTTERS. USE ONLY MEMORY WIRE CUTTERS OR YOU WILL HAVE LEARNED AN EXPENSIVE LESSON. TRUST ME, WOULD I STEER YOU WRONG?

3 create and attach dangles

Make three dangles as shown above using the following beads and findings: cream pearl and rondel crystal on a looped head pin linked to a large jump ring; jet crystal cross on two large jump rings; green pearl on a looped head pin linked to a large jump ring. Attach each dangle to a small jump ring and open and close the small jump ring to secure it to the covered memory wire.

4 attach end dangles

Slide a crystal teardrop, a khaki bicone and a jet round onto a ball-tipped head pin and make a coiled loop (see Bead Basics, page 20). Make a second identical dangle and attach one to each end of the necklace with a 4mm sterling jump ring.

the goods

- 2" (5cm) diameter dyed yellow shell pendant
- one each tiny fork, knife and spoon charms
- eight 10mm x 20mm brown rhodochrosite puffy rectangles (bacon beads)
- thirty-two approx. 9mm x 6mm dyed yellow freeform shell beads
- sterling hook and eye EZ crimp clasp
- twelve 4mm sterling jump rings
- eight 20-gauge sterling head pins
- 9-link segment SP extension chain
- 22" (56cm) strand of .018" (.45mm) 49-strand wire

the tools

- round-nose pliers
- chain-nose pliers
- crimp tool
- flush cutters
- bead board

sunrise special (NECKLACE)

inspiration
bacon and eggs

Now you can wear the most important meal of the day all day long. You — never know just what might inspire you once you begin looking at the world like an artist. How about breakfast, for starters? I found these beads in three different places, but somehow when they came together in my studio a funky design was born. Note the tiny silverware accents! This is a breakfast you won't need to work off at the gym, hurrah!

1 make bacon dangles

Slide each rectangle bead onto a head pin and make a coiled loop (see Bead Basics, page 20).

2 bead first half of necklace

Bead the necklace in the following sequence, beginning with four yellow shell beads: bacon bead on jump ring, three yellow shell beads. Repeat pattern four times. After the fourth cycle of the pattern, slide the yellow mother-of-pearl pendant onto a jump ring and slide the jump ring onto the wire. Continue beading in the established pattern, ending with four yellow shell beads.

ALWAYS USE A BEAD BOARD OR A BEAD MAT TO KEEP YOUR MATERIALS ORGANIZED. LAYING EVERYTHING OUT IN AN ORDERLY FASHION KEEPS YOU FROM SKIPPING BEADS WHEN STRINGING A PATTERN, AND KEEPS YOU FROM GETTING ANNOYED AT RUNAWAY BEADS.

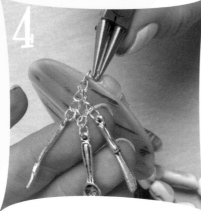

3 secure crimp clasp

At the end of the necklace, secure the wire with a crimp clasp. This clasp is secured by squeezing the straight sides together inside of the round section of your crimp tool. Trim away the excess tail with wire cutters.

4 attach utensils dangle

Separate out a nine-link section of chain and attach the fork charm to the third link with a 4mm jump ring. Skip one link over from the fork (center link), add the spoon and skip one link over from the spoon and add the knife. Attach the end of the chain back to the jump ring to make a circle. Secure the embellished chain to the jump ring on the pendant.

the goods

- peacock feather fringe on muslin tape, cut to length that fits neck
- five ½" (1cm) silver-plated Pacific opal Swarovski filigree components
- six 40mm x 20mm frosted black stone ridged beads
- size 16 SP snap fastener
- extra-strong black thread
- Aleene's Stop Fraying fabric glue or G-S Hypo Cement

the tools

- hammer - grommet-setting tool - scissors - heavy-duty embroidery needle (must fit through holes in beads) - bead mat (recommended) - measuring tape

vamp (CHOKER)

inspiration
peacock feather fringe

This dramatic feather and bead choker would make Theda Bara proud. Vampy, sassy and oh-so-divine! When I saw this peacock feather fringe, I just knew it would make a sensational choker. If you can sew with a needle and thread, then you can whip this bad girl up in a hot second. Paint some kohl around those baby blues, rouge those cheeks, apply crimson lips, roll down your stockings and grab a flask…then hear them all whisper, "Kiss me, you fool."

1 measure and cut feathers

Measure your neck with a measuring tape, holding the tape snug against your neck the way you like a choker to fit. Cut the peacock feathers to that measurement.

2 secure snaps

Secure the snaps on either end of the fabric strip that holds the peacock feathers with a grommet-setting tool and a hammer.

patience booster

THE FEATHER FRINGE IS STICKY, SO WORK SLOWLY AND USE SEVERAL SEPARATE THREAD SECTIONS RATHER THAN ONE LONG STRAND. YOU MAY WISH TO CLEAN THE NEEDLE AS YOU WORK WITH A "GOO" REMOVER.

3 sew on black beads

Thread a small needle that can fit through the hole in the black bead with black thread. Start at the end that receives the snap shaft and bring the needle up so that it is flush with the snap. Knot the end of the thread and sew the black bead onto the strip of muslin tape. Every black bead should be sewn through twice to make sure it's attached securely.

4 sew on filigree beads

Bring the needle back up through the muslin tape and sew on a square filigree. Continue sewing on the two kinds of beads, alternating between them. At the end, leave a little breathing room (about 1/8" [3mm]) between the last bead and the snap. Filigrees should be tucked slightly underneath the ends of the black beads. Use strong glue to bind the loose tape fibers on each end.

the goods

÷ ten 9mm x 6mm tanzanite Swarovski teardrops

÷ ten 12mm x 5mm dyed lavender jade rice beads

÷ eleven size 19 inside-color
Paula Radke dichroic beads

÷ ten 24-gauge sterling head pins

÷ twenty-one 20-gauge sterling
ball-tip head pins

÷ Paula Radke sterling bling ring

the tools

÷ round-nose pliers ÷ chain-nose pliers ÷ flush cutters

52

sea anemone bling (RING)

inspiration
sea anemones

Inspired by the opalescence, movement and magic of sea anemones, this big, bold ring is surprisingly comfortable. The purple rice-shaped beads wrap themselves around your finger and move almost organically. This is one of those times when I added a few more head pins than required, but I was delighted when I ended up with this fantastic cocktail ring! You may be cursing me as you try to fit this many pins onto the loops on the ring, but hang in there, baby, the end result is worth the strain!

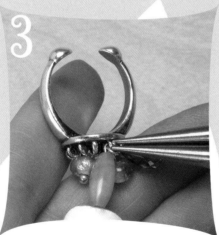

1 make beaded head pins

Make all of your dangles first. Use ball-ended head pins for the dichroic beads and the jade rice and the regular head pins for the tanzanite teardrops.

2 attach first beaded head pin to ring

Attach one of the dichroic dangles to the center loop of the ring using round-nose pliers and chain-nose pliers to secure it closed.

3 link three beaded head pins to one external link

Attach three dangles to one of the outside links of the ring: a round inside-color bead dangle, a teardrop dangle and a jade rice dangle, moving from the inside to the outside layer.

4 attach final head pin

Continue adding three beads to each ring link until you reach the final bead.

Patience booster

LOOK, DON'T MAKE YOUR-SELF CRAZY! THE LAST BEAD IS WELL-NIGH IMPOSSIBLE TO SECURE. IF THE NUMBER OF DANGLES I'VE USED SENDS YOU OVER THE EDGE, DELETE SOME BEADS. KNOW YOUR LIMITATIONS!

the tools

⁙ round-nose pliers ⁙ chain-nose pliers
⁙ flush cutters ⁙ bead mat

54

five easy (E A R R I N G S)

Earrings are one of the most quick and rewarding jewelry projects. Here the colors and themes are drawn from lovely Art Nouveau images. Art Nouveau artists were particularly interested in using nature as their source of inspiration, so why not take a cue from them and try venturing outside into the wilds of nature to see what might inspire you!

filigree flower earrings

the goods

- four 5mm x 4mm coral tubes
- two 8mm x 6mm lime green opaque Czech glass ovals
- eight 5mm x 6mm eggshell blue Czech glass teardrops
- two filigree flower chandelier earring components
- two 20-guage gold-plated head pins
- 24-gauge gold-plated craft wire
- 8mm diameter dowel or paintbrush handle

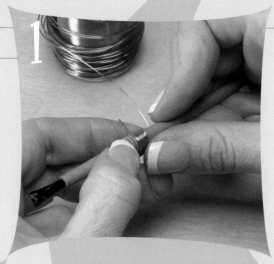

1 begin to make jump rings

Wrap wire around an 8mm paintbrush handle or a dowel rod.

2 cut coiled wire into jump rings

Slide the wire off of the paintbrush or dowel rod and use wire cutters to cut the coiled wire into jump rings.

3 create coral dangles

These little coral tube beads need 24-gauge wire to accommodate their tiny holes. Cut off four 1" (3cm) segments of wire with your flush cutters and slide each bead onto a length of wire. Make a loop working at the very end of the pliers. Make a second larger loop in the wire at the other end of the bead. Make a total of four coral dangles.

4 create all earring components and arrange

Make the remaining dangles for each earring: slide eight eggshell blue teardrops onto gold jump rings and two green Czech glass ovals onto head pins and turn a loop in the wire above them. Lay out all of your components and then use round- and chain-nose pliers to link them to the earring forms.

seafarer threader earrings

the goods

- ⸪ two 6mm smoky quartz Swarovski bicones
- ⸪ two 6mm erinite Swarovski briolettes
- ⸪ two 5mm aqua Swarovski side-drilled flower beads
- ⸪ two 20-gauge sterling ball-tip head pins
- ⸪ two 20-gauge sterling head pins
- ⸪ two 4mm sterling jump rings
- ⸪ two 2mm sterling jump rings
- ⸪ two sterling 5" (13cm) threader earring components

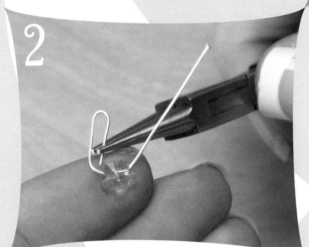

1 bend wire into U shape

Slide an aqua flower bead onto a silver head pin and bend the wire into a U shape.

2 bend wire back down

Use round-nose pliers to bend one side of the wire back down toward the bead.

3 wrap wire to create dangle

Wrap the remaining end of the wire around the doubled-up wire to create a loop. Make a second aqua flower dangle for the other earring. Use flush cutters to clip the excess wire tails.

4 assemble earrings

Make the remaining dangles for the earrings, two each of the following: an erinite briolette on a jump ring and a smoky quartz bicone crystal on a head pin with a wrapped loop. Attach each set of dangles to a silver jump ring and attach the jump ring to the end loop on the threader earrings.

gold etruscan bird earrings

the goods

- ⁙ two 10mm x 8mm faceted dyed purple jade ovals
- ⁙ four 4mm faceted mint green AB Czech glass rounds
- ⁙ four 6mm striated purple and green Czech glass rondels
- ⁙ two Etruscan vermeil bird clasps
- ⁙ eight 2mm gold-plated jump rings
- ⁙ ten 20-gauge gold-plated head pins
- ⁙ two gold-plated lever back earrings

1 remove component from clasp

Since I've repurposed this clasp as an earring component, you'll need to remove the toggle clasp and jump ring. The jump ring has been soldered, so you'll have to cut it off with wire cutters.

2 make dangles and assemble earrings

Slide each of the following beads onto head pins and make a wrapped loop in the wire above them: two faceted purple jade ovals, four striated green/purple rondels and four faceted AB mint green Czech rounds. Slide each dangle onto a jump ring and link the jump rings to the earring components. Link each purple jade oval directly to the center loop of the earring component. Link an earwire to the loop at the top of each component to finish.

earth flower earrings

the goods

- ⁙ two 8mm dyed green jade coin beads
- ⁙ two 8mm dyed orange jade coin beads
- ⁙ two 9mm carved dyed blue jade flower beads
- ⁙ two 6mm sterling ball beads
- ⁙ six 20-gauge sterling head pins
- ⁙ two star-tipped head pins
- ⁙ two sterling earwires

cathedral diamond chandelier earrings

the goods

- ⁙ six 4mm tourmaline Swarovski bicones
- ⁙ six 6mm purple velvet Swarovski rondels
- ⁙ two 6mm padparascha Swarovski briolettes
- ⁙ two two-section sterling chandelier earrings
- ⁙ two 6mm sterling jump rings
- ⁙ twelve 20-gauge sterling head pins
- ⁙ two sterling earwires

To make these long and slender chandelier earrings, simply slide each of the smaller beads onto a head pin and create a loop at the top of each. Slide the larger teardrop beads onto jump rings. Attach all of the beads to the chandelier components as shown.

To make these delicate dangles, simply thread each bead onto a head pin and turn a loop at the top. Attach the dangles to the chandelier components as shown. The center sterling bead goes on a star-tipped head pin. Make the two earrings mirror images of each other to create a left and right earring.

the goods

- thirty-six 6mm light topaz Swarovski briolettes
- thirty-six 20-gauge gold-plated head pins
- thirty-six 6mm gold-plated jump rings
- chicken feather trim on muslin tape
- black mini tote bag
- eighteen black wooden bracelet tiles
- Art Chix mini mix collage sheets
- magnetic snap
- Diamond Glaze
- découpage medium
- heavy-duty black embroidery thread

the tools

- sewing machine ÷ heavy-duty embroidery needle ÷ gold leafing pen
- scissors ÷ round-nose pliers ÷ chain-nose pliers ÷ flush cutters
- straight pins ÷ craft knife

58

"the ladies" (PURSE)

inspiration
chicken feather trim

Back in the day, many women kept small flocks of chickens in their back yards, and I highly recommend it in modern times as well. The women of yore referred to their chickens as "The Ladies." This chicken feather trim is an exact match to my dear chicken, Goldie. It seemed perfect for framing a jaunty little tote bag. Then I simply had to add these lovely vintage Ladies around the top and, of course, just a touch of sparkle.

1 pin feathers onto bag

Pin the feathers to the tote bag just beneath the doubled edge of the fabric.

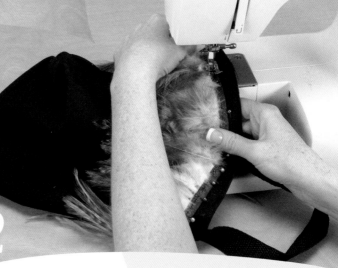

2 sew feathers onto purse

Sew the feathers onto the purse, carefully removing the pins as you go.

3 attach magnetic snap

Find the center point of the purse, lay the snap onto the purse and trace around it with a craft knife to cut out two holes for the prongs. Slide the cover over the prongs and bend the prongs down with pliers. Repeat for the other side of the tote.

4 cut out images for tiles
Use a craft knife to cut out the images you'll découpage onto the wooden tiles (these will be sewn onto the purse in a later step).

5 embellish image
Adhere each image to a wooden tile with découpage medium and allow the tiles to dry. Embellish each image with gold leafing pen.

6 apply diamond glaze
Apply Diamond Glaze to each tile with your finger, spreading it evenly. Allow the tiles to dry.

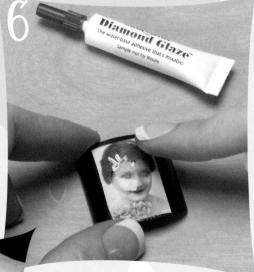

7 begin to sew tiles onto purse
Sew the tiles onto the purse over the strip of fabric that holds the feathers together. Double-sew through both of the holes in the wooden tiles. Make sure the tiles are aligned with the top of the chicken feathers.

8 add head pins to tiles

Slide a head pin through each of the holes in the tiles, from top to bottom. Turn a loop in the head pin wire.

9 link crystals to head pin loops

Slide each of the crystals onto a jump ring and link one jump ring with crystal to each head pin loop.

10 finish adding crystals

Continue adding crystals on jump rings to each tile.

"I would venture to warn against too great an intimacy with artists as *it is very seductive and a little dangerous.*"

—Queen Victoria

"Silly things do cease to be silly if they are done by sensible people in an impudent way."

—Jane Austen

Prim and Proper Ladies

(designs inspired by Victorian and Art Nouveau images)

all hail.

DEAR READER,
WHEN COMMENCING A
THOROUGH EXAMINATION OF
DESIGN ELEMENTS from the turn of the last century, you
must remember always to maintain an aura of great dignity and rever-
ence for the past. A true lady refrains from exuberant outbursts of delight or loud
noises of any kind, to be certain. The richness of the design elements from this period of
time (when everything was completely and deliciously over the top, whilst maintaining a
surface level air of absolute calm) offers a treasure trove of ideas to the artist. Prepare to
be overwhelmed by the overstuffed, while you discover a delightful world of inspiration.

the inside
Scoop

The designs in this chapter come from Victorian and Art Nouveau images. Though my

personal aesthetic is more streamlined, I am intrigued by the strange combination of repres-

sion and rigid social etiquette with a sexually charged subtext that marks the art from this

era. The wonderful colors in the hand-tinted photographs from this time period, particularly of

women in Grecianesque costumes surrounded by kooky props, offer wonderful design starting

points. Look for ornate findings, chains, filigree and highly ornamented beads, add five

more things than you think you need, and there you have it, Victoriana.

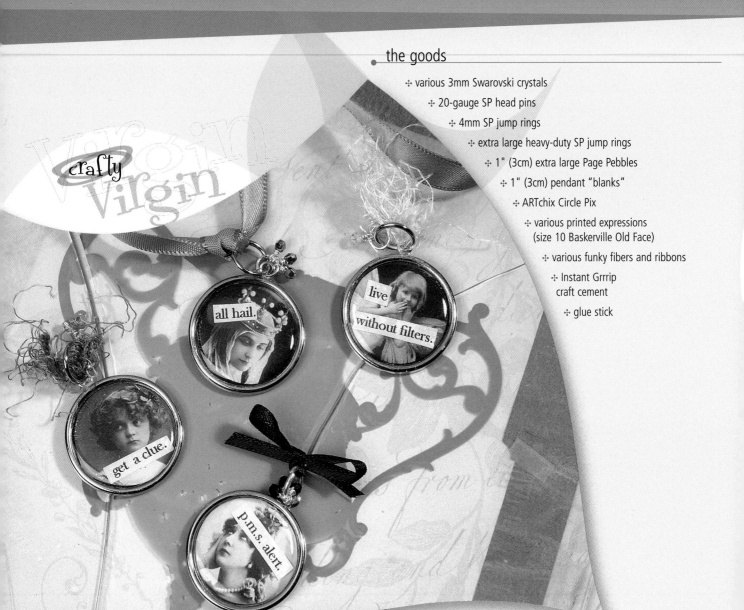

the goods

- various 3mm Swarovski crystals
- 20-gauge SP head pins
- 4mm SP jump rings
- extra large heavy-duty SP jump rings
- 1" (3cm) extra large Page Pebbles
- 1" (3cm) pendant "blanks"
- ARTchix Circle Pix
- various printed expressions (size 10 Baskerville Old Face)
- various funky fibers and ribbons
- Instant Grrrip craft cement
- glue stick

crafty Virgin

all hail.

live without filters.

get a clue.

p.m.s. alert.

the tools

- craft knife ⁘ cutting mat ⁘ round-nose pliers
- flush cutters ⁘ chain-nose pliers ⁘ scissors

pms (PENDANTS)

Some days every girl has a little attitude, and so be it. When you are full of — spit and vinegar, throw on one of these pendants and let the world be forewarned! I am crazy about these ephemera images from ArtChix Studio. They rock! Yippee! All you need are some beads, glue, fibers and a printer. Oh, and just a dash of sarcasm. Snark.

1 cut out phrase

Type up a list of words and phrases that go with the images you chose for this project and print them out. Choose a phrase and cut it out.

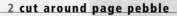

MAKE THESE INTO NECKLACES OR PINS BY USING DIFFERENT FINDINGS. I AM LEAVING THAT ALL UP TO YOU—NOW GO OUT THERE AND BE CREATIVE!

2 cut around page pebble

Adhere the cut-out word to the Page Pebble with a glue stick and then lay the pebble on top of the circular image you choose. Cut around the pebble with a craft knife.

3 apply instant grrrip glue

Squirt a little Instant Grrrip glue into the silver frame and spread it around evenly in a thin coat.

4 adhere page pebble

Put the Page Pebble into the frame, pressing down on it to adhere it to the backing.

5 tie bow

Cut a small piece of ribbon and tie it in a bow around a link in the chain attached to the silver frame. If you like, make a couple of beaded dangles and link those to the chain as well. Make a "bail" by attaching an extra large jump ring to the top of each pendant.

the goods

- six 8mm faceted tiger's eye coins
- six 13mm x 7mm diamond turquoise beads
- eight 14mm x 10mm textured sterling beads
- 25mm carved bone monkey pendant
- two 11-link sections of large sterling silver chain
- large textured sterling silver toggle clasp
- four heavy-duty 10mm sterling jump rings
- eight 22-gauge ball-ended sterling head pins
- twelve 22-gauge sterling head pins
- textured SP watch face

the tools

- round-nose pliers ∻ chain-nose pliers ∻ flush cutters

66

monkey in the middle (CHARM WATCH)

inspiration
coats & clark ad and beads

The lovely muted colors in this old Coats & Clark advertisement gave me the idea for this snazzy little watch. I chose the carved bone monkey pendant to mirror both the texture and color from the ad. The combination of turquoise and tiger eye stones has just the right mix of earth and water. Simply charming, wouldn't you agree?

1 cut off wire sections

Use wire cutters to cut off the linked chain into two sections of 11 links each.

2 attach chain link sections to watch face

Double the chain and attach the center link to the watch face with a jump ring, using your pliers to secure it in place. Repeat for the remaining 11-link section of chain on the other side of the watch face.

3 begin to attach dangle to chain link

Slide a bead onto a ball-ended head pin and turn a loop above the bead as for a wrapped loop (see Bead Basics, page 20). At this stage, slide the loop onto a link in the chain.

4 finish wrapped loop

Finish attaching the dangle to the link by wrapping the tail of the wire around the base of the loop. Trim away excess wire with wire cutters. Continue to attach dangles to the chain in the same manner in the following pattern on the bottom section: diamond turquoise bead, textured sterling bead, tiger's eye coin, sterling bead, diamond turquoise. On the top section, follow this pattern: tiger's eye, sterling, turquoise, sterling, tiger's eye. (Turquoise beads go on plain head pins, and tiger's eye beads and textured sterling beads go on ball-ended head pins.)

5 attach monkey bead to finish

Slide the monkey bead onto a ball-ended head pin and make a wrapped loop. Open the jump ring by which the chain is attached on the top of the watch and slide the dangle onto it. Close the jump ring to secure the monkey dangle. Add your clasp using a jump ring to secure the toggle to both beaded chains. Repeat on the other side.

the goods

- four pink frosted lucite crystal flowers
- ten 6mm blue faceted lucite rounds
- 9mm x 6mm aqua Swarovski teardrop
- two 3mm light rose Swarovski rounds
- two 6mm crystal AB Swarovski rondels
- six 4mm striated pink Czech glass rondels
- four size 2 crimp tubes
- two heavy-duty 6mm sterling jump rings
- crystal heart toggle clasp
- crystal chandelier component
- textured watch face
- 2" (5cm) thin blue ribbon
- two 5" (13cm) lengths Beadalon .018" (.45mm) 49-strand wire
- Aleene's Stop Fraying glue

the tools

- round-nose pliers ÷ chain-nose pliers ÷ crimp tool
- flush cutters ÷ scissors ÷ bead mat

pretty in pink (W A T C H)

inspiration
victorian ad

A romantic Victorian advertising image provided me with the watercolor — pastel tones and slightly over-the-top design elements for this watch. Egads, a girl is never too old to be pretty in pink. This is the perfect accessory for those prim and proper ladylike occasions. Add a high-necked lacy blouse and Gibson Girl hairstyle, then offset the top of your outfit with some well-fitted jeans and high heels. Now grab a copy of Emily Post and head out for high tea. Good day to you, miss.

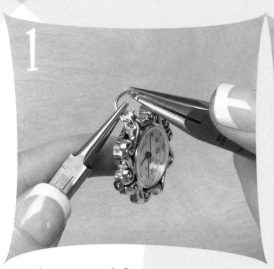

1

1 change watch face

Use your pliers to remove the existing D-rings from the watch face. Replace them with sturdy sterling jump rings.

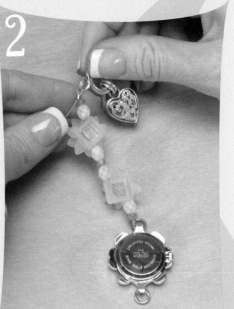

2

2 bead first half of watch

Attach a wire to one of the jump rings with a crimp tube. Bead the wire in the following sequence: Pink rondel, blue faceted bead, pink flower, blue faceted bead, pink rondel, blue faceted bead, pink flower, blue faceted bead, pink rondel. Be sure to note that the wire threads through the pink flowers diagonally. Crimp the end of the wire to the loop of the circle half of the toggle clasp. Bead the second half of the watch in the same way.

69

3

3 make dangle

Add some beaded dangles to a chandelier component and attach the dangle to the jump ring on one side of the watch face.

4 tie on dainty blue bow

Cut a small piece of narrow blue ribbon and tie it in a bow to the free jump ring connected to the watch face. Add a dab of glue to the ends of the ribbon to prevent fraying.

take it from me

OF COURSE, I REALIZE THIS IS A COMPLETELY IMPRACTICAL DESIGN, BUT FEAR NOT! THIS WATCH IS FOR SPECIAL OCCASIONS, MY DEAR. YOU CAN WEAR SOMETHING THAT "TAKES A LICKING AND KEEPS ON TICKING" ON THE WEEKDAYS!

4

the goods

- two 3mm light peach Swarovski bicones
- two 3mm chrysolite Swarovski bicones
- two 3mm crystal AB Swarovski bicones
- six 20-gauge SP head pins
- 6mm SP jump ring
- metal lock and key charm
- sheer blue thin ribbon
- vintage optometrist's lens
- circle images collage sheet
- computer-printed phrase in Baskerville Old Face, 10 point
- Mod Podge glossy
- Omni-Gel transfer medium
- glue stick
- bowl of water

She Walks in Beauty

❖❖❖❖❖❖❖❖

*She walks in beauty,
like the night,*

*Of cloudless climes and
starry skies;*

*And all that's best
of dark and light,*

*Meet in her aspect
and her eyes...*

—*Lord Byron*

the tools

- scissors or craft knife
- disposable paintbrush
- round-nose pliers
- chain-nose pliers
- flush cutters

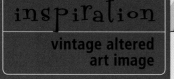

she walks in beauty (PENDANT

Who doesn't love a bad boy poet like Lord Byron? Imagine yourself a Romantic era muse when you sport this lovely antique optometrist lens pendant. Honestly, this came about after I screwed up and was ready to start over. Just then, voilá, it was perfect. Never, ever be afraid to make mistakes.

1 cut out phrase

Type up some poetic phrases and print them out. Cut one phrase out with a craft knife. Also cut out an image to fit the diameter of your optometrist's lens.

2 glue phrase onto image

Glue the cut-out phrase onto the image.

3 adhere image to lens

Adhere the image with its phrase onto the back of the optometrist's lens with Omni-Gel transfer medium. Let the medium dry.

4 peel off backing

Moisten the back of the paper with water and peel off a little of the paper backing. Be careful and go slowly as you peel. If you're too vigorous, you will accidentally peel the whole thing off and have to start over. When the paper has dried, seal it with a coat of Mod Podge glossy.

5 attach charms and beads to lens

Link a jump ring to the optometrist's lens and then attach charms and beads to the jump ring.

6 thread lens onto ribbon

Cut two lengths of light blue organza ribbon and thread them both through the metal loop at the top of the optometrist's lens. Tie a knot in each end of the ribbon.

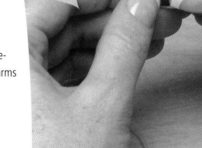

the goods

+ two 8mm faceted green-blue Czech glass windowpane beads
+ ninety-six 10mm x 5mm striated opaque aqua Czech glass fish beads
+ forty-two 14mm x 10mm faceted aquamarine glass ovals
+ one hundred ninety-two size 14 inside-color turquoise seed beads
+ one hundred ninety-two size 11 sage seed beads
+ one hundred ninety-two size 11 inside-color green seed beads
+ two sterling Bali cones
+ two 20-gauge sterling eye pins
+ four 4mm sterling jump rings
+ oval textured sterling toggle clasp
+ twelve size 2 crimp tubes
+ six 20" (51cm) lengths of .010" (.25mm) 49-strand wire

the tools

+ round-nose pliers + chain-nose pliers
+ crimp tool + flush cutters + bead mat

my bonny lies over the ocean (NECKLACE)

inspiration
WWI image

Strand after strand of lovely aqua, blue and sea green beads cascade from — Balinese sterling silver cones in this substantial monochromatic necklace. A touching image of a mother and child awaiting the return of their soldier during WWI provided the subtle shades of blue, and the ocean theme is echoed in the tiny kissing fish beads. Whether you wear this necklace twisted or with the strands hanging individually, you'll be striking.

1 attach wire to eye pin

Open a jump ring and slide an eye pin onto it. Close the jump ring to secure the eye pin. Attach one wire to the jump ring with a crimp tube (see Bead Basics, page 16).

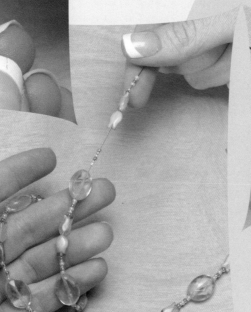

2 string first strand

String the first strand of beads in the following pattern: sage seed bead, turquoise seed bead, green seed bead, sage, turquoise, green, two fish beads (nose to nose), green seed bead, turquoise seed bead, sage seed bead, green, turquoise, sage, aquamarine oval. Repeat the pattern seven times, ending with the first seed bead sequence.

3 attach first beaded wire to eye pin

Attach the end of the first beaded strand to a jump ring linked to an eye pin, as in step one. Repeat steps one through three for the remaining five strands.

4 thread eye pin through cone

Thread one of the beaded eye pins through the bottom of a sterling cone, pulling the strands flush to the top of the cone.

5 coil wire on top of bead

Add a green-blue windowpane bead to the exposed end of the eye pin and use two pliers to secure and wrap a coiled loop at the top of the bead. Grasp the loop with one set of pliers after forming the loop and hold it steady while wrapping the end in a tight coil with a second set of pliers. Repeat for the other side of the necklace. Attach the toggle clasp to the ends of the necklace.

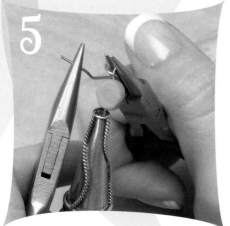

❖ thirty-three 5mm rose Swarovski rounds

❖ thirty-five 5mm jonquil Swarovski rounds

❖ 2mm crystal AB Swarovski Hot Fix crystals

❖ white long-sleeved heavyweight t-shirt

❖ fabric transfer images

❖ white beading thread

❖ fabric glue

❖ butterfly stamp

Vixen
crafty Vixen

the tools

❖ sturdy needle (with small eye) ❖ Hot Fix crystal applicator
❖ fabric glue (Fabri-Tac Adhesive) ❖ fabric markers ❖ fine-tip
permanent marker ❖ scissors

fly (T-SHIRT)

inspiration
vintage ephemera fabric images

This little girl is so adorable, I used her image twice in this book. I love the colors that tint this photograph and the priceless expression of ennui on her face. The butterfly theme is carried through on the stamps along with the pretty colors. Sometimes we all need to be reminded that life is most rewarding when we are willing to take a few risks, drop our baggage, spread our wings and fly.

1 adhere image to shirt

Cut out the fabric image you choose and glue it to the bottom left corner of the t-shirt with fabric glue. Allow it to dry.

2 sew beads around image

Thread a needle with a long piece of white thread. Thread all of the beads for one row onto the thread. Then bring the needle back through the beads, stitching through every two to four beads to tack them to the shirt.

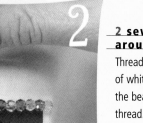

3 stamp black butterflies onto shirt

Use a Fabrico marker to apply black ink to a butterfly stamp and stamp butterflies in a diagonal line from the bottom corner to the top. You may also use a fine-tip permanent marker to go over the butterfly images to fill in details. Clean your stamps thoroughly.

IF YOU ARE A WIZARD WITH PHOTO TRANSFERS, CREATE YOUR OWN IMAGE TO ATTACH TO THE SHIRT. YOU CAN TAKE ANY OF THESE PROJECTS AS FAR AS YOUR CREATIVE HEART WILL GO…

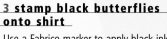

4 stamp colorful butterflies onto shirt

Apply color to the butterfly stamps and stamp the colored butterflies over the black butterflies. Stamp the butterflies at varied angles so they look like they're in motion.

5 draw swirls on t-shirt

Use a fine-tip permanent marker to handwrite "fly" in cursive. Draw in some ornamental swirls to accent the butterflies.

6 adhere crystal accents

Apply crystal accents to the butterflies and to the image using the Hot Fix crystal applicator.

⁘ four 8mm heliotrope center-drilled Swarovski flowers

⁘ four 3mm black diamond AB Swarovski rounds

⁘ fabric transfer fairy image

⁘ washable felt in pink, fuchsia, lime, blue and purple

⁘ bright blue 8-strand DFN embroidery floss

⁘ dark thread

⁘ fabric glue

crafty
goddess

the tools

⁘ sewing needle (eye must fit through crystals)

⁘ scissors ⁘ black pen

auntie flo's pretty little (TAMPON CASE

inspiration

felt and Victorian images

Let's face it, most of us carry around a tampon or two in our purses. After a while, they get totally destroyed. I have to give credit to the genius Vinnie for coming up with the original tampon case. Pink and purple felt and a campy Victorian image make this a more feminine version. Keep mad money, tampons, a mini chocolate bar, some aspirin, whatever you need, in this discreet pouch. Maybe it will make you feel a little better when you see Auntie Flo is keeping your womanly needs in check.

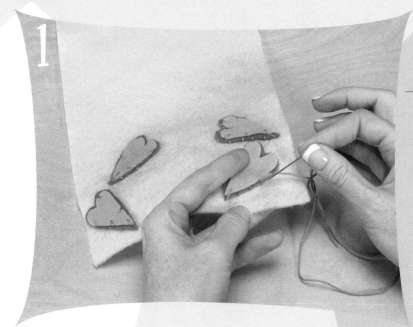

1 sew layered hearts onto pink felt

Cut a piece of light pink felt to 12" x 61/4" (30cm x 16cm). Use the templates to create hearts out of fuchsia and lime felt. Layer the smaller green hearts on top of the larger hot pink hearts and sew them using a whip stitch to the bottom third of the light pink felt with electric blue embroidery floss. (The back gets covered up, so you don't have to worry about making it look super neat.)

2 whip stitch around heart

Cut out four small hot pink hearts and whip stitch around each heart with electric blue embroidery floss.

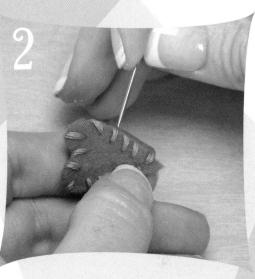

Hearts and stars are shown at full size.

3 glue hot pink heart on top of layered hearts

Use fabric glue to adhere a small pink heart on top of the two layered hearts. Allow it to dry.

4 sew beads onto hearts

Thread a needle with a length of dark thread. Thread a crystal flower and a black diamond round onto the thread and sew them to the center of each heart. You can use pliers to pull the thread through the layers of felt if it's hard to push the needle through with just your fingers.

5 sew stars onto pink felt

Make a copy of the star templates onto stiff paper and cut them out. Trace around them onto the felt and cut out the stars. Sew the layered stars onto the pink felt with a whip stitch using blue thread.

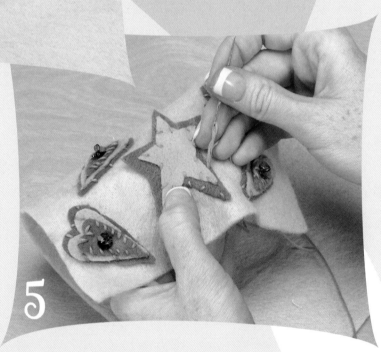

6 adhere image to square

Cut out one of the images from the fabric transfer sheet and glue it onto a small hot pink square of felt. Glue the image to the center of the stars with fabric glue.

7 embroider letters

Cut a purple piece of felt to 12¼" x 6¼" (31cm x 16cm). Write the phrase "seek chocolate" in black permanent marker in the top third of the felt rectangle. Thread a needle with blue embroidery floss and stitch over the letters with a chain stitch.

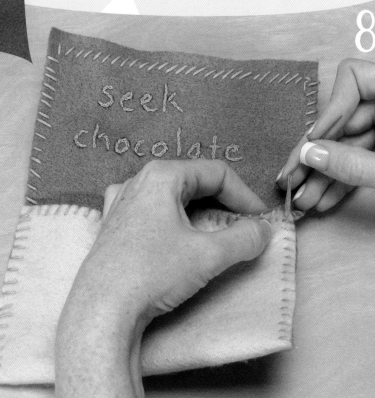

8 stitch purple and pink felt together into pouch

Lay the purple felt on top of the pink felt so that the bottom and side edges are even and the purple felt is a little taller than the pink along the top edge. Fold up the bottom third of the layered felt rectangles to create the pouch. Use blue embroidery floss to stitch the two pieces of fabric together. Conceal the knots inside the pouch.

Especially FOR You

80

Jazz Babies, Swingsters, Bobby Soxers, and go-go girls

designs inspired by 1920s, 30s, 40s, 50s, and early 60s kitsch

LISTEN
HERE, GIRLIE,
YOU MAY THINK YOU'RE THE
BEE'S KNEES…but I am here to tell you that
your grandma had her day too. I bet you never pictured her
rolling down her stockings, bobbing her hair, sipping from a flask and
riding in a rumble seat…23 skidoo! Whatever you are doing that you think is
so new and cool, I can guarantee you some seemingly innocent little old lady already
did it first. Don't forget to pay a well-deserved tribute to the trailblazers who paved the
way with their rebellion to make it easier for you to do the same. We really have come
a long way, baby, and many of our sassy older sisters paid the dues and then paid them
forward. Long live Rosie the Riveter. We can do it!

the inside
scoop

This chapter explores a myriad of design motifs, colors and images from the 1920s through

the 60s. Designs from these eras will help to spark a bevy of fun and kitschy design ideas.

Whether you pull your inspiration from preassembled collections or get out there and

rummage at the thrift shops and antique stores, the images you'll discover from these eras

encapsulate the mood of our culture as it moved from the Art Deco period through the pop

art movement of the early 60s. You may be surprised at how fresh and new some of

these ideas will feel to you.

- **gmp pancake earrings**
  ‡ four 4mm jonquil AB Swarovski bicones
  ‡ two 6mm crystal copper Swarovski rounds
  ‡ two 6mm turquoise Swarovski bicones
  ‡ four 4mm light Siam Swarovski bicones
  ‡ two light Siam crystal chandelier components
  ‡ twelve 20-gauge SP head pins
  ‡ two 4mm SP jump rings
  ‡ two SP flat coil earwires

- **little miss earrings**
  ‡ two 6mm peridot AB Swarovski bicones
  ‡ four 4mm jonquil Swarovski bicones
  ‡ four 4mm indicolite AB Swarovski bicones
  ‡ two peridot crystal chandelier components
  ‡ ten 20-gauge SP head pins
  ‡ two SP flat coil earwires

- **happy day earrings**
  ‡ two 9mm x 6mm tanzanite Swarovski teardrops
  ‡ four 6mm hyacinth Swarovski bicones
  ‡ four 5mm crystal AB Swarovski rounds
  ‡ two tanzanite crystal chandelier components
  ‡ ten 20-gauge SP head pins
  ‡ two SP flat coil earwires

- **lithiated lime earrings**
  ‡ four 6mm peridot AB Swarovski bicones
  ‡ two 6mm jet Swarovski rondels
  ‡ two 4mm fire opal AB Swarovski bicones
  ‡ two 4mm peridot AB Swarovski bicones
  ‡ two 4mm jonquil AB Swarovski bicones
  ‡ ten 20-gauge SP head pins
  ‡ two 20-gauge SP eye pins
  ‡ two 4mm jump rings
  ‡ two jet crystal chandelier components
  ‡ two SP flat coil ear wires

the tools

‡ round-nose pliers ‡ chain-nose pliers ‡ flush cutters ‡ bead mat

82

advertastic (CHANDELIER EARRINGS)

inspiration
vintage labels

Vintage labels from the 1930s and 40s were the inspiration for the colors — in these crystal and metal chandelier earrings. I love the unexpected but delightful color combinations they provided. Advertising art is an excellent source for striking color combinations, since it is created specifically to catch the eye.

gmp pancake earrings

To make these earrings, create looped, coiled or double-looped head pins as shown (see Bead Basics, pages 18–21). Attach a dangle to each of the three loops in the chandelier component: jonquil, copper, jonquil. Attach a jump ring to the copper rondel and link three more dangles to the jump ring: light Siam, turquoise, light Siam. To finish, add a flat coil earwire to the top of each earring.

happy day earrings

Create the looped dangles as shown by turning a loop in the head pin wire above each bead. Attach the crystal dangles to the chandelier component using round- and chain-nose pliers in the following order: crystal round, hyacinth bicone, tanzanite teardrop, hyacinth, crystal. Add flat coil earwires to the top of each earring to finish.

little miss earrings

Create the looped dangles as shown by turning a loop in the head pin wire at the top of each bead. Attach the dangles to the chandelier component using pliers in the following sequence: indicolite, jonquil, peridot, jonquil, indicolite. Add the flat coil earwires to the top of each earring to finish.

lithiated lime earrings

Create looped head pins with the 6mm and 4mm bicone beads. Coil the head pins above the beads. Slide the jet rondels onto eye pins and create double-looped segments. Link the crystals to the chandelier components as shown, dangling the three 4mm beads on jump rings attached to the 6mm jet rondels.

the goods

✤ twenty-six plastic bubblegum charms (4 Scottie dogs, 4 doghouses, 6 skulls, 7 boots, 5 lanterns)

✤ SP toggle clasp

✤ twenty-seven extra heavy-duty large silver-plated jump rings

✤ 7" (18cm) length large SP link chain (13 links)

the tools

✤ round-nose pliers ✤ chain-nose pliers

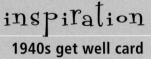

84

get well good luck (CHARM BRACELET)

A festive get well card from the 1940s was the springboard for the vibrant — colors in this gumball charm bracelet. Somehow, I just couldn't stop adding these happy plastic charms. You won't be able to sneak up on anyone in this one…so it is not recommended for playing hide and seek. But for playing dress up, well, this is perfect…hello!

1 attach toggle clasp to chain

Attach the circle end of the toggle clasp to one end of the chain. Open the chain link as shown, using round- and chain-nose pliers or two pairs of chain-nose pliers.

2 link first two charms to chain

Slide each charm onto a jump ring. Attach one charm to each side of the first link by opening and closing the jump ring around the link.

take it from me

IF CHUNKY PLASTIC CHARMS DON'T RING YOUR CHIMES, SUBSTITUTE SMALLER DANGLES. OR, TRY THIS ONE ON FOR SIZE AND TAKE IT OUT FOR A SPIN. YOU MAY BE SURPRISED HOW MUCH FUN YOU HAVE!

3 finish attaching charms

Continue attaching two charms to each link of the bracelet. Attach the bar end of the toggle clasp to the final chain link with a jump ring. Adding the jump ring to the clasp will help it to fit through the circle end of the clasp when the bracelet is worn.

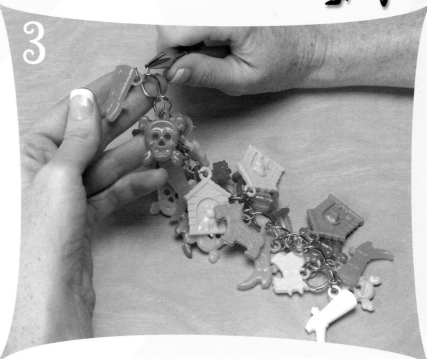

the goods

- ❖ four 18mm x 12mm aquamarine Swarovski polygons
- ❖ three aqua and black diamond SP Swarovski filigree flowers
- ❖ four 14mm Bermuda blue Swarovski open squares
- ❖ four 14mm crystal Swarovski open squares
- ❖ four 14mm cream Swarovski pearls
- ❖ forty-six 6mm crystal AB Swarovski rondels
- ❖ 24-gauge colourcraft silver-plated wire
- ❖ wire-tooth metal headband (Goody)

the tools

❖ wire cutters ❖ chain-nose pliers

enchanted (TIARA)

With its springtime motif and many shades of blue, this 1940s Easter card — made me think of a fanciful garden where flowers of crystal might grow and twinkle in the sun. My botanical vision lead me to create a sparkling tiara. Follow the pictures in your own head—let them lead you down the unexpected garden path.

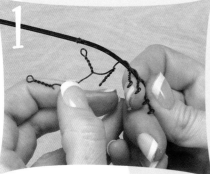

1 remove teeth from headband

Clip the teeth from the headband at one end using flush cutters, and then unwrap the teeth.

2 wrap plain crystals

Cut a 20" (51cm) section of wire and wrap it several times around one end of the headband. Thread a crystal rondel onto the wire. Wrap the beaded wire around the headband, keeping the bead at the top. Wrap five more crystals onto the headband, maintaining tension on the wire.

3 twist wire for first "garden flower"

Thread an open-square bead onto the wire, about 1¼" (3cm) above the headband. Wrap the wire around the square at least four times to secure it. Then loop the wire around the headband. Grasp the square between thumb and forefinger and slowly twist the wire clockwise. Continue twisting evenly until the wire is secured. Don't overdo it or the wire will break.

patience booster

AS YOU WRAP BEADS ONTO THE HEADBAND, YOU MAY RUN OUT OF WIRE. IF THIS HAPPENS, JUST ADD NEW WIRE. CAREFULLY TUCK THE ENDS OF THE WIRE INTO THE HEADBAND WITH PLIERS AS YOU WORK.

4 twist on polygon bead

Twist on two crystal rondels as in step two. Twist on a crystal open-square bead slightly higher than the first square, followed by two more rondels. Slide a polygon bead onto the wire and bring it flush to the top of the headband. Fold the wire flush to the back of the bead and wrap it around the headband, leaving a small bit of wire exposed at the base of the bead. Twist the bead once to secure it flush against the headband.

5 bend flower to secure it

Wrap two more rondels around the headband. Then twist on a cream pearl, folding the wire against the back of the pearl and then twisting it to secure the bead. Wrap on two more rondels and thread the wire through an opening in one of the petals of a crystal flower. Wrap the wire around the headband and twist it to secure the bead as before. Bend the flower over, flush to the wire stem, to secure it.

6 finish beading tiara and curve stems

Continue wrapping beads onto the headband in the established pattern until you reach the center filigree flower, which should be the highest point on the tiara. Work the second half of the tiara in a mirror image of the first half. To finish, wrap the wire around the headband several times and tuck the tail under with pliers. Curve the wire stems as desired.

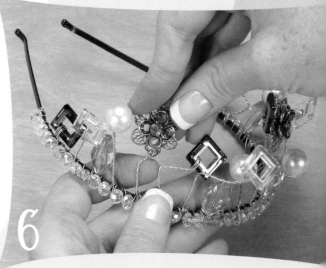

÷ fifteen plated brass charms (5 21mm x 20mm small arrow, 5 20mm x 12mm small pear, 5 26mm x 11mm short marquise)

÷ fifteen 6mm sage Swarovski Hot Fix or flat-back crystals

÷ three tonally similar printed papers (mini stack value pack)

÷ fifteen 4mm SP jump rings

÷ small SP toggle clasp

÷ 17½" (45cm) elongated steel chain

÷ Mod Podge glossy

÷ Instant Grrrip craft cement two-part epoxy (optional)

crafty Vixen

MAKE THE SCENE

the tools

÷ disposable paintbrush ÷ electric bead reamer ÷ Hot Fix crystal applicator (or tweezers) ÷ scissors or craft knife ÷ chain-nose pliers

agent 99 (NECKLACE)

inspiration

atomic-themed tags and papers

Sometimes you come up with something so cool, you just have to jump for joy. —— Making a lot of crap often precedes the jumping-for-joy part, but hey, it's all part of the journey. When I saw these atomic 50s metal shapes, ooooohhhhh, was I excited. Then I found these fantastic color-coordinated retro scrapbook papers and a cool design started brewing in my head. I love the retro atomic era look of this design. This necklace is perfect for the beatnik in all of us—grab your bongos and head to the coffee house.

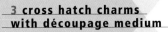

1 glue metal charms to paper

Position each metal charm on top of an area of decorative paper that will work with each shape. Then turn the paper over and glue each charm down with Instant Grrrip craft cement.

2 cut around metal shapes

Cut around each metal charm with a craft knife or scissors. Repeat steps one and two to cover the other side of the charm with paper.

3 cross hatch charms
with découpage medium

Use a small paintbrush to apply découpage medium to each charm going in one direction. Allow it to dry. Apply another layer of découpage medium with a paintbrush, cross hatching in the other direction to create texture. Once the medium is dry, use an electric bead reamer to drill through the paper at the hole in each charm.

4 adhere crystal accents to charms

Use a Hot Fix crystal applicator to adhere a crystal accent to each charm, or if you're using regular flat-back crystals, you can glue the crystals on with two-part epoxy, using tweezers to pick up and place the crystals.

5 attach charms to chain

Attach the charms to the linked chain with jump rings. Begin attaching charms at the eleventh link from the end, starting with a marquise-shaped charm, then a small arrow-shaped and a pear-shaped charm, ending with a marquise-shaped charm. Attach a charm every fourth link. Use pliers to attach the toggle clasp to the last link on each end of the chain.

the goods

- **tote**
  - ❖ tote bag pattern from Simplicity (It's So Easy 5151, bin 9)
  - ❖ one yard cotton pin-up boy fabric
  - ❖ one yard yellow cotton broadcloth liner
  - ❖ twelve snaps size 16
  - ❖ one set round bamboo handles
  - ❖ thread

- **beaded handles**
  - ❖ one hundred sixty large dyed coral chips
  - ❖ eight lampwork beads
  - ❖ ten 12mm x 10mm pyrite beads
  - ❖ two small SP toggle clasp circles
  - ❖ two SP swivel lobster clasps
  - ❖ two size 2 crimp tubes
  - ❖ .018" (.45mm) 49-strand wire

the tools

❖ sewing machine ❖ needle ❖ hammer ❖ grommet-setting tool ❖ crimp tool ❖ flush cutters ❖ scissors ❖ bead board

pin-up boys (PURSE)

inspiration
pin-up boys fabric

Retro pin-up girls may be everywhere these days, but let's give the boys their due, shall we? The beach boys on this sassy fabric are adorably dorky and instantly lovable. I've added snaps to this simple-to-sew tote bag so you may switch it up and change your handles (as often as you change your men, dare I say?). You can wear the funky beaded handles as necklaces when you sport the bamboo handles.

1 sew body of purse

Follow the Simplicity pattern to sew the body of the purse as shown.

2 put on first snap

Attach the first snap to the purse as shown in the diagram on this page using a grommet-setting tool and a hammer. Make sure to measure and mark your snap placement before you commit them to the fabric.

3 snap wooden handles into place

Continue to secure all of the snaps in place with the grommet setting tool and the hammer. When the snaps are in place, snap each of the wooden handles into place.

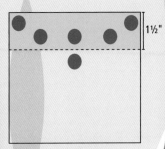

1½"

•SNAP PLACEMENT
Fold and pin fabric to 1½" (4cm). Attach center top snap under folded fabric with prong facing inside of bag. Attach remaining snaps as shown, checking handles for exact locations before attaching.

4 string handles

If you'd rather have beaded handles, create your own in colors that coordinate with your fabric. Crimp a toggle circle to a long piece of wire with a crimp tube. String beads on in the following pattern: pyrite bead, eight coral chips, lampwork bead. Crimp a swivel lobster clasp to the end.

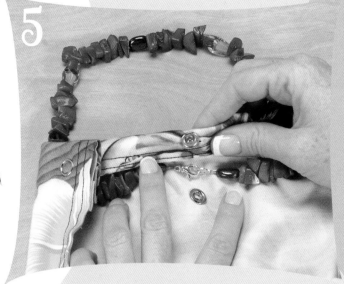

5 snap handles into place

Snap the beaded handles into place to change the look.

the goods

÷ twelve 8mm crystal Swarovski cubes

÷ twelve 8mm black diamond Swarovski cubes

÷ twenty-five 4mm olivine diagonal Swarovski cubes

÷ twenty-five 7mm gray AB Czech glass squovals

÷ seventy-five 3mm light rose AB Swarovski rounds

÷ seventy-five gunmetal head pins

÷ seventy-five gunmetal eye pins

÷ fifty-two gunmetal jump rings

÷ small SP toggle clasp

the tools

÷ chain-nose pliers ÷ round-nose pliers
÷ flush cutters ÷ bead mat

domestic diva (NECKLACE)

inspiration
vintage apron

If you don't thrift shop, my dear, you are missing out on a world of inspiration—and it often comes cheap, mind you. The color scheme in this crystal-laden necklace comes from the cutest vintage apron I picked up at the local Goodwill. I pulled gray, pink and green from the floral fabric and translated them into crystals. The kooky 1950s colors are perfect for this choker fit for Scheherazade...just add seven veils. Think Mrs. Cleaver goes to Persia. Get out there, roll up those sleeves and rummage!

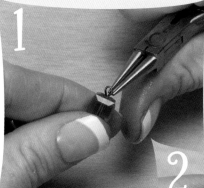

1 make dangles

Thread the crystal cubes onto eye pins and make a loop at the top of each one with round-nose pliers (see Bead Basics, page 18). Continue to make all of the dangles you'll need for the necklace: 75 wrapped loop 3mm light rose dangles; 25 double-looped squovals; 12 black diamond double-looped cubes; 12 double-looped crystal cubes; and 25 olivine double-looped diagonal cubes.

2 create first segment

The "main" part of the necklace is made up of double-looped black diamond cubes and crystal cubes linked with jump rings. Dangles constructed of a double-looped olivine diagonal cube, and a double-looped squoval linked to a jump ring with three wrapped-loop 3mm light rose rounds hang from the jump rings that connect the larger crystal cubes. See the diagram for construction details.

take it from me

IF YOU LIKE HOW I USED THE COLORS IN THE VINTAGE APRON IN THIS NECKLACE DESIGN, YOU COULD TRY COMING UP WITH YOUR OWN DESIGN BASED ON A FABRIC YOU LIKE. A GOOD BOOK ON VINTAGE FABRICS AND STYLES WILL HELP YOU BECOME AN EXPERT IN NO TIME.

3 continue linking segments and finish necklace

Continue building and linking beaded segments, alternating between black diamond and crystal cubes. When all of the beaded segments are linked together, attach the toggle clasp. Check back through your work to make sure all jump rings and loops are secure.

8mm crystal Swarovski cube

8mm black diamond Swarovski cube

gunmetal jump ring

4mm olivine diagonal Swarovski cube

7mm gray AB Czech glass squoval

gunmetal jump ring

3mm light rose AB Swarovski round

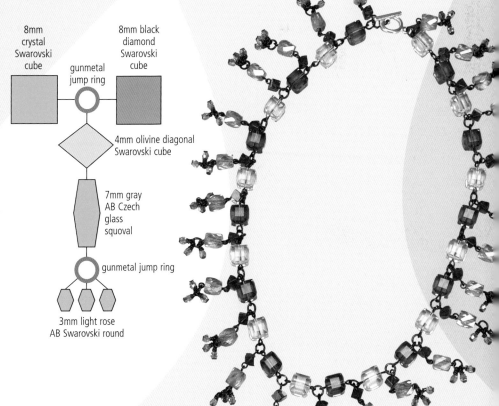

- thirty-seven indicolite Swarovski square channels
- thirty-six rose Swarovski square channels
- thirty-seven olivine Swarovski square channels
- three large-hole top-drilled gold-plated circles
- three extension chains with lobster clasp (attached to final jump rings)
- one hundred and fifteen 6mm gold-plated jump rings

crafty Virgin

Virgin

the tools

- chain-nose pliers - round-nose pliers

94

(you) go-go girl (NECKLACE)

Remember Joey Heatherton—the singer-actress-turned-Serta Perfect Sleeper - spokeswoman? I adored her. This flashy gold necklace was inspired by a funky 1960s jumpsuit Joey would have been right at home in. To make this design, I pulled pink, teal and olive green from the pattern on the jumpsuit. The design elements have a retro feel, but these long wrap-around styles are making a big comeback. Wrap this neck candy twice, three or even four times and let the charms fall in front or back.

1 link first three channels in pattern

Link the crystal channels together with gold jump rings in the following pattern: blue, pink, green. Continue linking the channels until you've used them all.

2 remove lobster clasp

Remove the lobster clasps from each of the gold extension chains by opening the jump ring by which they are attached.

3 attach discs to extension chains

Open and close a jump ring to attach a gold disc to each extension chain.

4 attach extension chain with lobster clasp

Add a lobster clasp and the three extension-chain dangles to a jump ring and link the jump ring to one end of the necklace. Add a second jump ring to the other end of the necklace.

⁘ microscope slides

⁘ vintage magazine

⁘ pin/pendant component

⁘ copper tape (silver-tone)

⁘ lead-free white solder wire

⁘ various chains, ribbons and clasps
for necklace chains

crafty
goddess

serial shopper

shoe

mood

PLAY

the tools

⁘ craft knife ⁘ cutting board ⁘ two-part epoxy
⁘ soldering iron ⁘ burnisher/bone folder ⁘ glue stick

96

under the microscope (PIN OR PENDANT

As soon as I saw this fantastic idea, I just had to give it a whirl—never mind that I had no idea how to solder! To make this pin and pendant combo, I simply sandwiched an image between two microscope slides and soldered them together. Vintage advertisements from old women's magazines and the cheeky, ironic copy that accompanies them are the perfect punny inspiration. Don't be afraid to try new techniques—you really can do it!

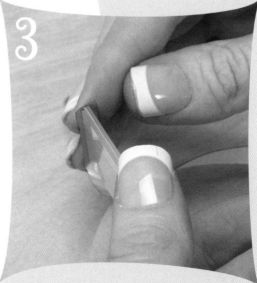

1 cut out face

Place a cutting mat under the page of the magazine with the image you chose. Place a microscope slide on the page over the portion of the image you'd like to use. Cut around the slide with a craft knife. Find a word or phrase you'd like to include and cut that out as well.

take it from me

I LOVE TO SEARCH FOR TREASURES AT ANTIQUE STORES—OLD MAGAZINES ARE FAIRLY EASY TO FIND AND VERY AFFORDABLE. YOU CAN FIND PRESIZED VINTAGE MICROSCOPE SLIDE IMAGES AT SEVERAL OF THE ALTERED ARTS WEB SITES LISTED IN THE RESOURCE SECTION IF YOU AREN'T FEELING ADVENTUROUS.

2 glue phrase onto image

Glue the phrase onto the cut-out image with a glue stick.

3 sandwich image between microscope slides

Clean the slides—make sure you remove all spots from the glass that will be facing the "inside." Sandwich the image between two glass microscope slides.

4 adhere copper tape to slides

Cut off a length of copper tape and secure the microscope slides together with it. Try to make sure that the tape stays centered along the edges of the slides. Go over the copper tape with a bone folder to make sure it's well adhered to the glass.

5 solder copper tape

Plug your soldering iron in and wait for it to heat up. Touch the tip of the hot iron to the solder wire—it will melt on contact and stick to the tip of the iron. Touch the tip of the iron to the copper tape on the slide and work slowly along its surface, applying the solder to one small area at a time.

6 clean glass

Use a craft knife to clean up any of the solder residue that might have stuck to the glass.

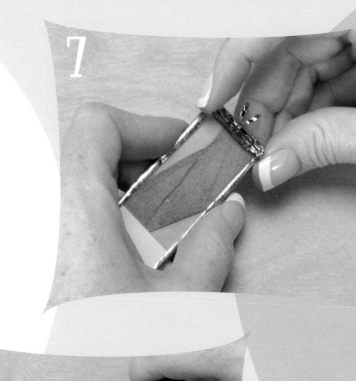

7 attach pendant to microscope slides

Use two-part epoxy to attach the pendant to the back of the soldered microscope slides.

8 add chains

To make the microscope slides into a pendant, string it onto a length of chain. Simply add a toggle clasp to the end of the chain.

the goods

- ⊹ black shelf-bra tank top
- ⊹ fabric image transfer sheet
- ⊹ small piece of white fabric
- ⊹ three red plastic beehive beads
- ⊹ two amber plastic beehive beads
- ⊹ two hundred and forty-one 2mm black diamond Hot Fix Swarovski crystals
- ⊹ red cotton thread
- ⊹ fabric glue

crafty
goddess

the tools

⊹ Hot Fix crystal applicator wand ⊹ scissors ⊹ sewing needle
⊹ cardboard section for inside tank top ⊹ fine-tip fabric marker

her story (TANK TOP)

inspiration
vintage scarf

Have you ever wondered what it might be like if women had written the history books? How different would the focus be? What stories would we share? I bet they would be fascinating. Here is a tribute to the idea of finally telling Her Story. I pulled the color combination for this feminine tank from this swirly vintage scarf that's soft but also strong and bold.

1 cut out image

Select the image you'd like to use from a sheet of fabric transfers and cut it out with scissors. Leave a small border around the image.

2 write on fabric

Cut out a small rectangle of white fabric and write the phrase of your choice on it using a black fine-tip fabric marker.

3 glue image and phrase onto tank

Slide a piece of cardboard or a thick sheet of paper inside the tank top to protect it from glue. Use fabric glue to adhere the image and the phrase to the shirt. Let the glue dry overnight.

4 begin to adhere crystal border

Use the Hot Fix crystal applicator to adhere a double border of Hot Fix crystals along the edge of the image.

5 finish crystal border

Finish the crystal edging with a single border around the phrase.

6 sew on bead accents

Sew the red and gold beads onto the top of the tank, sewing back through each bead multiple times (10 or 11 times).

"I've been
absolutely
terrified
every moment
of my life—
and I've never
let it keep me
from doing a
single thing I
wanted to do."

—Georgia O'Keeffe

"The only people who never
tumble are those who never mount the
high wire. This is your moment. Own it."

—Oprah Winfrey

Brave New Girls

funky designs using and inspired by non-bead items

ARE YOU READY
TO MOUNT THE
HIGH WIRE, to defy convention, to find a brave new world
of inspiration? Now that we have paid tribute to the past, we are setting
forth into the future. Now's the time to smash that glass ceiling and start com-
manding your own reality. Be not afraid—you have to let go of the past in order to
grab the future. I will help you navigate the first few steps, but after that, it is totally
up to you!

In this final chapter you will be introduced to some unconventional techniques and

sources of inspiration. The idea here is to give you a push into a new perspective on design,

to show that you absolutely can find inspiration virtually anywhere and to help expand your

crafty universe beyond the bead. From the hardware store to the laboratory to the vast wealth

of inspiration from other cultures…you are officially invited to get out there and explore. I,

for one, can't wait to find out what you discover! Are you ready, Thelma?

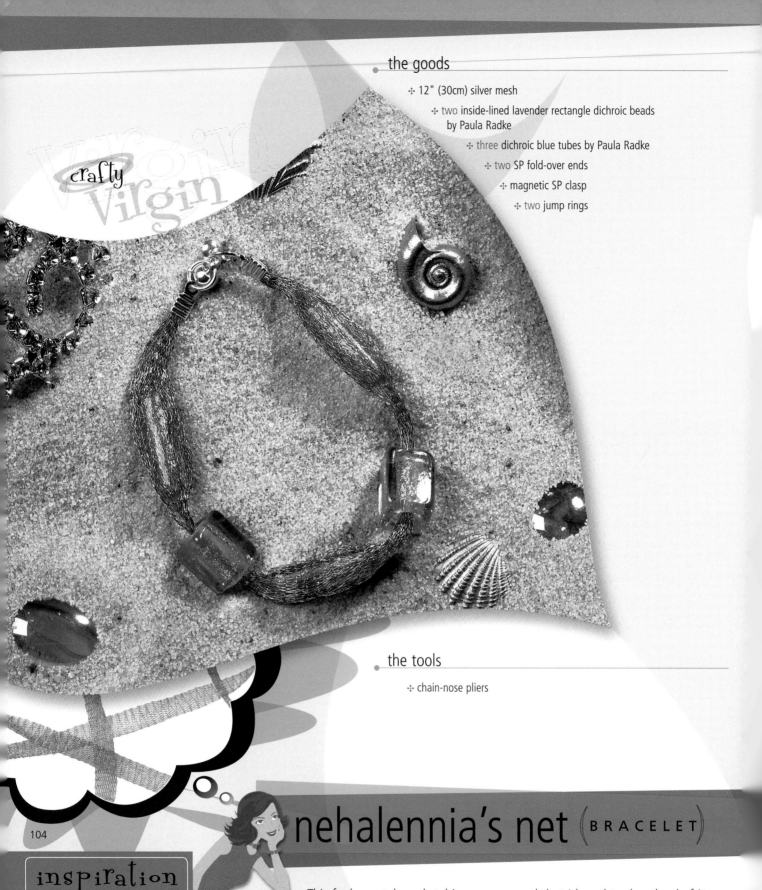

- 12" (30cm) silver mesh
- two inside-lined lavender rectangle dichroic beads by Paula Radke
- three dichroic blue tubes by Paula Radke
- two SP fold-over ends
- magnetic SP clasp
- two jump rings

crafty Virgin

the tools

- chain-nose pliers

104

nehalennia's net (BRACELET)

inspiration
metal mesh tubing

This funky metal mesh tubing was so cool that I bought a boatload of it. The possibilities are endless with this stuff. Feel free to bend it, shape it, stick stuff in it, thread stuff on it…need I go on? When matched with the iridescence of dichroic glass and crystal, the results are positively luminous. In case your curiosity was piqued, Nehalennia is a Celtic goddess of the sea.

1 attach mesh to fold-over end

Lay one end of the mesh on top of a fold-over end and fold one arm over the mesh using chain-nose pliers. Repeat for the other arm of the fold-over end.

2 insert bead into mesh

Open the mesh tubing and slide a bead inside of it.

3 thread bead onto mesh

Twist the mesh up to make it fit through the hole in a second bead and continue to twist the mesh as you pull it through the bead. You may even need to grab the mesh with pliers to pull it through. As dichroic beads are handmade, some holes are bigger than others. Alternate between inserting beads into the mesh and threading the mesh through beads.

ALWAYS BE ON THE LOOKOUT FOR INTERESTING NEW MATERIALS. NOW THAT YOU HAVE ENTERED THE TERRITORY OF THE BRAVE NEW GIRL, YOU ABSOLUTELY HAVE TO BREAK THE MOLD!

4 attach clasp to free end of mesh

Attach the clasp with a jump ring to each of the fold-over ends.

the goods

✣ Zombie String Gang™ doll
✣ freshwater pearl cross
✣ two Siam 6mm top-drilled Swarovski bicones
✣ two 5mm AB crystal Swarovski rounds
✣ sterling Patience medallion
✣ five sterling ball-ended head pins
✣ six 4mm sterling jump rings
✣ sterling key chain

the tools

✣ round-nose pliers ✣ chain-nose pliers ✣ flush cutters

zombie boy (KEY CHAIN)

inspiration
zombie boy doll

This little string doll is a fair trade handicraft from Thailand, and I just couldn't resist his quirky charms. I modified him slightly and gave him an enormous necklace to remind myself to try to find patience…which can be particularly challenging whilst driving! Making crafts is like cooking. You don't always have to start from scratch—add and alter to doctor up purchased items.

1 attach sterling key chain to string doll

Remove the ball chain from the top of the string doll's head using round-nose and chain-nose pliers. Attach the last link in the silver key chain to the metal ring.

2 attach dangles to top of key chain

Make dangles with the two Siam 6mm bicone crystals and attach them to the last link in the key chain.

3 Attach patience medallion

Make a couple of dangles and slide them onto the ball chain. Slide the patience medallion onto the ball chain as well and fasten the chain around the doll's neck.

take it from me

THIS DOLL IS MADE FROM ONE CONTINUOUS PIECE OF STRING. TRY YOUR HAND AT CREATING A LOVABLE MONSTER OF YOUR OWN, IF YOU DARE!

the goods

⁘ variety of crystal components
⁘ variety of crystal beads
⁘ flip-flop charm and other charms
⁘ scrapbook stickers (two for each charm)
⁘ 4mm SP jump rings
(three for each charm)
⁘ lobster clasps

the tools

⁘ electric bead reamer ⁘ round-nose pliers
⁘ chain-nose pliers ⁘ flush cutters

scrappy chick charm (PENDANTS

Best Friends

Her majesty

Overdressed again!

Glam!

Oh Baby!

Happy Birthday!

Chocolate!

Quee

inspiration
scrapbook stickers

I admit it, I am not "scrappy." It just is not my thing, probably because of — my innate "procrastinative" (yes, I know it is not a word) tendencies. But I do love the cool products in the scrapbook aisles! These adorable retro plastic stickers were begging to become charms, so I stuck them back to back and drilled a hole with my handy-dandy bead reamer and voilà! Add on some color- and theme-coordinated sparkles, charms and crystal components and now we're talking!

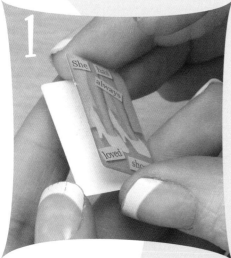

1 stick scrapbook stickers back to back

Select two scrapbook stickers with similar themes and colors. Line them up and stick them together back to back.

2 drill hole with bead reamer

Drill a hole in the top right corner with a bead reamer.

3 attach charm with jump rings

Attach the scrapbook charm to a chandelier earring component using three jump rings in a chain formation (the chain allows the charm to dangle nicely from the bottom ring). Attach the other charms or beads you selected with jump rings to the chandelier component.

take it from me

DON'T STOP AT ONE—
THESE LITTLE GUYS ARE SO FUN AND EASY
TO MAKE, YOU CAN THROW TOGETHER
A BATCH AT A MOMENT'S NOTICE. NIFTY
GIFTIES FOR YOUR GAL PALS!

4 attach clasp

Add a lobster clasp on a jump ring to the top of the charm. (This makes a cool clip-on charm you can then attach to whatever you desire!)

the goods

- two **extra large** clear resin stickers
- two **medium** clear resin stickers
- handmade **embellished** paper
- ten **4mm** SP jump rings
- two **sterling** ball French earwires

the tools

- craft knife ⁑ cutting mat ⁑ electric drill
- round-nose pliers ⁑ chain-nose pliers

pretty papers (E A R R I N G S)

inspiration
handmade papers

I had a blast in the scrapbook aisles, if you can't tell. A girl simply must expand her repertoire! Resin page stickers with pretty paper sandwiched in between make funky beads in a flash. These textured and stamped handmade papers remind me of Indian saris. The possibilities are endless here…so go forth and create freely!

1 place resin stickers on paper

Select the area of the paper you'd like to highlight for your earrings, and place the resin sticker on the paper.

2 cut out paper circle

Cut around the resin stickers with a craft knife.

3 adhere second resin sticker

Adhere a second resin sticker to the back, sandwiching the paper in the middle.

4 drill holes in resin stickers

After marking the center points on the resin stickers, use an electric drill with a small drill bit to make a hole in the top and bottom of each smaller resin sticker sandwich, and in the top only of the large resin sticker sandwiches. Repeat steps one through four to make as many resin stickers as you'll need for your earrings.

take it from me

YOU CAN USE ANY SORT OF PAPER HERE THAT TICKLES YOUR FANCY. TRY NEWSPAPERS, SUNDAY COMICS, MAGAZINES, STAMPED IMAGES. FREE YOUR CREATIVE MIND!

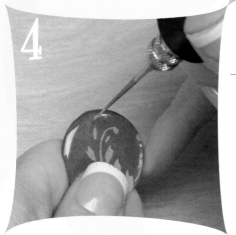

5 link resin stickers

Link the resin stickers together with jump rings and attach the top page pebble to an earring wire. Repeat to make a second earring.

the goods

- ✧ seven-tile blank black wooden stretch bracelet
- ✧ textured pink fiber paper
- ✧ three small Asian-themed stamps
- ✧ .8mm clear Elasticity
- ✧ black inkpad (StazOn)
- ✧ Mod Podge glossy
- ✧ gum arabic
- ✧ metallic gold and red Pearl Ex powder pigments
- ✧ sixteen Swarovski jet hematite m-foiled flower Hot Fix crystals
- ✧ G-S Hypo Cement

the tools

- ✧ Hot Fix crystal applicator wand ✧ disposable paintbrush
- ✧ scissors ✧ paint mixing plate

112

raku stretch (BRACELET)

inspiration
raku pottery

● I've always loved Raku pottery—but why should the shimmery, mottled surfaces of Raku pieces be limited to vases and serving platters? You can't wear a vase or a serving platter…at least not comfortably. When I saw this delicate Asian-style stamp and these airy textured handmade papers, I got to thinking that Raku might just look great in a bracelet. So I stamped, découpaged and dabbled until I came up with a fun little stretch bracelet.

1 stamp on textured paper

Stamp an Asian-themed image with black ink onto textured paper. Cut the textured paper into irregular straight-sided shapes that will fit onto the wooden tiles.

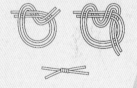

TO TIE A DOUBLE OVERHAND KNOT (OR A SURGEON'S KNOT), SIMPLY FOLLOW THE DIAGRAM. YOUR FINISHED KNOT SHOULD LOOK LIKE THE PICTURE ON THE BOTTOM.

2 découpage paper onto tiles

Remove the bracelet tiles from the fabric-coated stretch strand. Adhere the irregularly shaped papers to the tiles with découpage medium.

3 paint wooden tiles

Mix Pearl Ex powders and gum arabic. Use your finger to paint each wooden tile with the colored mixture to add texture.

4 add crystal accents

Use the Hot Fix tool to add a Hot Fix crystal accent to each wooden tile.

5 string tiles on elastic

String the wooden tiles onto two pieces of heavyweight elastic. Tie the ends of each piece of elastic together in a double overhand knot. Trim the ends of the elastic. Apply a dab of G-S Hypo Cement to each knot to secure them. Allow the glue to dry.

the goods

⁜ nine gold-tone metal butterfly-shaped doll house hinges
⁜ two 11" (28cm) lengths 1.5mm black leather
⁜ two 6mm gold-plated jump rings
⁜ large gold-plated toggle clasp
⁜ four 1.8mm glue-on cord ends
⁜ G-S Hypo Cement

the tools

⁜ round-nose pliers ⁜ chain-nose pliers

she's come unhinged
(B R A C E L E T)

inspiration
miniature doll house hinges

My husband is a closet designer. No, he doesn't design closets, he just doesn't want anyone to know he can make great jewelry. He really has an amazing design sense. I promised him I wouldn't tell that he created this ingenious bracelet for my book. So, don't tell him I told you, okay? Ha. Isn't this the coolest idea? I love it! These are actually hinges used to make miniature dollhouses. Thanks, honey, you are the best!

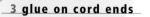

1 thread hinges on leather
Tie a knot at one end of each piece of 11" (28cm) long leather.
Thread all of the hinges onto the leather strands.

2 knot leather at ends
Knot each strand of leather to secure the hinges in place.

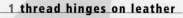

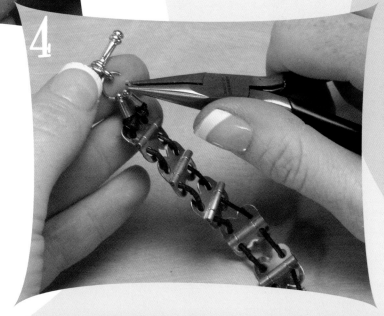

take it
from
me

HEY, YOU CRAFTY
CHICK READING THIS BOOK—WHY NOT
TAKE A TRIP TO THE LOCAL HARDWARE
STORE TO SEE WHAT FUNKY NEW ITEMS YOU
CAN COMMANDEER FOR YOUR JEWELRY
MAKING? DON'T FORGET THAT YOU'RE A
WHIZ WITH A SOLDERING TOOL NOW!
OOOHHH, SO MANY POSSIBILITIES!

3 glue on cord ends
Glue cord ends onto each end of each strand of
leather with G-S Hypo Cement. Allow the glue
to dry.

4 add jump rings and toggle clasp
Finish the bracelet by adding the bar end of a
toggle clasp to one end and the circle end to
the other end of the bracelet using jump rings.

the goods

- two 6mm rose top-drilled Swarovski bicones (for earrings)
- 6mm aqua, peridot and jonquil Swarovski bicones (1 of each color)
- nine vintage bottle caps in various colors
- five metal chick charms
- fifteen 6mm SP jump rings
- fourteen 10mm SP jump rings
- two sterling French earwires
- 16" (41cm) segment medium stainless steel curb chain
- small SP toggle clasp

the tools

- straight edge - crayon - small drill bit - drill or electric bead reamer - round-nose pliers - chain-nose pliers

crafty chick's bottle caps
(N E C K L A C E   A N D   E A R R I N G S)

inspiration
vintage bottle caps

Bottle caps have been used in design since at least as far back as the Tramp Art of the Great Depression. These outsider artists used found objects (okay, trash… they had to work with what they could get) to make amazing and intricate folk art. Several modern jewelry designers specialize in wonderful jewelry using vintage bottle caps. I wanted to try my hand at working with them, and somehow this cute little vintage chick charm seemed the perfect complement.

1 mark center of bottle caps

Using a crayon and a straight edge, mark the top and bottom center point on each bottle cap.

2 drill holes in bottle caps

Use an electric drill with a small drill bit to drill a hole in the top and bottom center of each bottle cap at the spots you marked in the first step.

take it from me

IF YOU USE BOTTLE CAPS WITH EDGES THAT HAVE NOT BEEN PRE-FLATTENED AS THESE HAVE, YOU WILL NEED TO USE A RUBBER MALLET TO CRIMP, OR FLATTEN, THE EDGES SO THEY LOOK LIKE THE CAPS IN THESE PHOTOS. IF YOU DON'T FLATTEN THE EDGES, YOU'LL HAVE A VERY SCRATCHY NECKLACE! OUCH.

3 create bottle cap pendants and link to chain

Link three bottle caps together with 10mm jump rings for the center waterfall dangle of the necklace. Create two more waterfall dangles of two bottle caps each. Attach the longest waterfall dangle to the center link of the chain with a large jump ring. Add the two shorter dangles, each 11 links from the center, with large jump rings. Make three crystal dangles and link a crystal and a chick charm to a jump ring. Link each chick and crystal dangle to the bottom bottle cap of each waterfall section with an extra large jump ring. Make some cute matching earrings using the same materials.

- 3mm jet Swarovski round
- 6mm crystal AB Swarovski round
- Premo! polymer clay in yellow, orange and blue
- gunmetal eye pin
- 30" (76cm) red polka dot thin grosgrain ribbon
- Mod Podge glossy

crafty Vixen

Vixen

- sharp pointed metal clay tool ÷ pasta machine
- toaster oven ÷ disposable paintbrush
- clay slicing blade ÷ chain-nose pliers

118

p. ducky (PENDANT)

inspiration
rubber duck bath toy

What is it about rubber duckies? They are so damn cute! I have tons of rubber duckies in my bathroom at home, and I just had to have a rubber ducky project in the book. Somehow, as this little ducky came to life, it seemed to be begging for a pageboy hat and a blingtastic crystal necklace. I had absolutely no control over this one! Ha. Thus, P. Ducky was born.

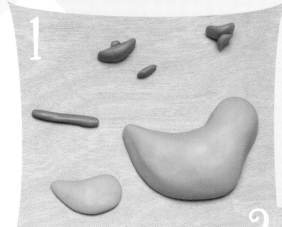

1 create duck body and accessories

Condition yellow, orange and blue clay by rolling it through the pasta machine in small slices. Then knead small bits of clay in your hands to soften the clay up further. Mold the clay into a duck body, a wing, a beak, a tiny beret with bill and a necklace. See photo.

2 assemble duck

Press all of the parts of the duck together lightly so the different clay parts adhere together.

REMEMBER, ONCE YOU USE A PASTA MACHINE FOR CLAY, YOU CANNOT USE IT TO MAKE FOOD. IT'S ALSO A GOOD IDEA TO DEDICATE A TOASTER OVEN EXCLUSIVELY TO POLYMER CLAY USE. THIS IS WHAT THE MANUFACTURER RECOMMENDS, AS DO ALL OF THE BIG POLYMER CLAY ARTIST TYPES. THE CLAY ISN'T TOXIC…BUT…YOU WOULDN'T WHIP UP AN OMELET WITH YOUR BEAD REAMER, OR WOULD YOU?!

3 add crystals

Push a small black crystal into the ducky's face to make an eye and add a crystal to the center of his necklace as well.

4 make feathers with clay tool

Create impressions in the wing with the clay tool that has a long pointed end. Before baking the duck, insert an eye pin into the top of the duck's head with chain-nose pliers. Bake the duck, following the baking instructions on the clay package.

5 thread ducky onto ribbon

After the duck has cooled, paint a thin layer of glossy Mod Podge onto him with a disposable paintbrush. Try to avoid painting over the crystals. Allow the découpage medium to dry. Thread a piece of narrow ribbon through the eye pin sticking out of the ducky's head and knot it to finish P. Ducky.

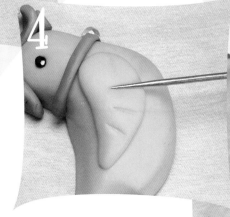

❖ four 5mm light Siam Swarovski rounds

❖ two 6mm crystal Swarovski butterflies

❖ Premo! polymer clay in white, yellow, orange, green and red

❖ five gunmetal eye pins

❖ two gunmetal jump rings

❖ two gunmetal head pins

❖ metal pin back

❖ Sparkle Mod Podge

❖ two-part epoxy

the tools

❖ pasta machine ❖ toaster oven ❖ various metal clay tools (Lowell Cornell 11 pc. clay set) ❖ chain-nose pliers ❖ round-nose pliers ❖ wire cutters ❖ clay blade ❖ disposable paintbrush

crafty Vixen

Vixen

120

day of the dead skull (PIN)

inspiration
calaveras (skulls) fabric

I have a true affinity for all things Mexican kitsch. When my husband and I had a retail — shop, we sold a ton of fun Day of the Dead folk art. In fact, we had the good fortune to travel to Oaxaca and Taxco to buy directly from the artists there. This funky vividly colored sugar skull fabric provided the roadmap for a polymer clay skull pin. I couldn't resist adding crystal earrings and some Sparkle Mod Podge. If you love a little humor with your Halloween time fun, this is the perfect project for you. This has the "kid seal of approval," courtesy of my seven-year-old daughter.

1 condition clay

Cut several slices of white clay with a clay blade and run them through the pasta machine. Repeat with all of the colors you'll use to decorate the skull: orange, yellow, green and red.

2 make skull

Knead the conditioned white clay with your hands and form it into a ¾" (2cm) thick, flat-backed oval. Press the bottom third of the oval in on both sides to make a chin and mouth area. Use the template on this page as a guide.

3 make nose indentation

Use a trowel-shaped tool to create two indentations in the skull for nostrils.

4 make teeth impressions

Use a sharp pointed tool to impress lines into the clay to create teeth.

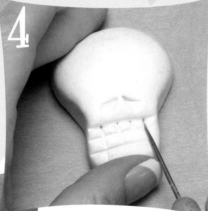

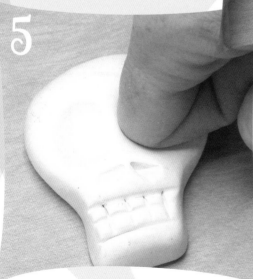

5 create eye indentations

Press the knuckle of your index finger into the clay skull to create eye indentations.

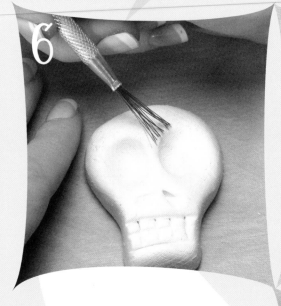

6 cross hatch skull to add texture

Using a tool that looks like a small metal broom, lightly impress the skull with cross hatch markings.

7 add eyebrows and lips to skull

Roll out several skinny tubes of orange clay, two for the eyebrows and two for the lips. Lay the eyebrows in curves that follow the eye sockets and curl one end of each upward a bit. Press the clay gently into the skull to adhere it. Repeat to make the lips.

8 apply yellow balls around eye sockets

Roll yellow clay into tiny balls. Press the balls around the eye sockets, flattening each one slightly.

9 create flower

Flatten a small amount of red clay on your work surface until it is very thin. Use your index finger and thumb to roll it up into a rose.

patience booster

I BURNED MY FIRST ROUND OF POLYMER CLAY PROJECTS WHEN WORKING ON THIS BOOK, SO I HIGHLY RECOMMEND YOU MONITOR THE CLAY CLOSELY WHILST IT BAKES. OR YOU CAN CHOOSE TO DISCOVER, AS I DID, HOW TO MAKE VERY REALISTIC LOOKING FAKE DOGGIE POO. EEK!

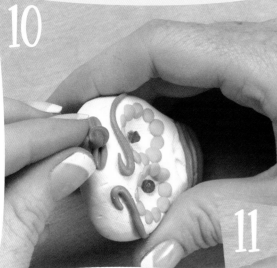

10 place flower and leaves

Carefully place a small red crystal into each eye socket and impress them gently into the clay. Roll green clay into two very small tubes with one pointed end and one more rounded end to make leaves. Flatten the leaves and adhere them to the top of the skull. Make an indention in the center of each leaf with the pointed clay tool. Place the red rose on top of the leaves and press down gently to adhere it.

11 place eye pins for ears

Push an eye pin into the skull on either side at about ear level using chain-nose pliers. Bake the clay according to the instructions on the package. Allow the skull to cool.

12 coat with sparkling découpage medium and attach earrings

Use a small paintbrush to coat the skull with Sparkle Podge. Avoid getting podge on the crystals. Allow the podge to dry. To make the earrings, create double-looped eye pins with the butterfly beads and attach single-looped head pins with the light Siam rounds to them. Connect the earrings to the "ears" on your skull with jump rings.

13 adhere pin back to skull

To finish the pin, adhere a pin back to the back center of the skull with two-part epoxy. Allow the epoxy to dry overnight.

resources

Most of the supplies used to make the projects in this book can be found in your local craft, hobby, bead, fine art or discount department stores. If you have trouble locating a specific product, contact one of the supply sources listed below to find a local or Internet vendor, or to request a catalog. Many of the suppliers listed generously donated product for this book.

Anita's™ Stamps
www.docrafts.co.uk
rubber stamps

ARTchix Studio
250.478.5985
www.artchixstudio.com
• altered arts supplies, ephemera photo fabric and paper collage sheets, and extraordinary artistic inspiration (Canada)

Auntie's Beads
866.26.BEADS
www.auntiesbeads.com
• beads, findings and stringing materials

Beacon Adhesives, Inc.
800.599.3400
www.beacon1.com
• Fabri-Tac glue

Beadalon
914.699.3405
www.beadalon.com
• 7-, 19-, 49-strand beading wire, stringing materials, findings, tools, Toho seed beads, Paula Radke beads, gemstone and glass beads

Blue Moon Beads/
Westrim Crafts
800.377.6715
www.bluemoonbeads.com
• beads and findings

Bond Adhesives
973.824.8100
• Instant Grrrip craft cement

Coats & Clark
800.648.1479
www.coatsandclark.com
• sewing and needlework products

CPE The Felt Company
800.327.0059
www.cpe-felt.com
• felt

Craft-Inc.
800.8-CRAFT8
www.craft-inc.com
• specialty dollhouse and craft metal hardware

Crystal Innovations/
Pure Allure, Inc.
800.536.6312
www.pureallure.com
• crystal and metal sliders, clasps, Swarovski crystal beads

Darice
866.4.Darice
www.darice.com
• craft supplier supreme

DFN
Designs for the Needle
Janlynn Products
800.445.5565
www.janlynn.com
• needle arts, scrapbooking, rubber stamps and more

Die Cuts With a View
801.224.6766
www.diecutswithaview.com
• scrapbooking supplies

Duncan
800.438.6226
www.duncan-enterprises.com
• glues, paints, ceramics, general crafts

Eastern Findings, Inc.
800.332.6640
www.easternfindings.com
• fabulous findings

EK Success, Ltd.
www.eksuccess.com
• pick-and-point color wheel, wide variety of craft and scrapbook supplies

Elvee Rosenberg Inc. and
Gampel Supply Inc.
212.575.0767
www.elveerosenberg.com
• imported novelty beads and other jewelry supplies

Euro Tool, Inc.
800.552.3131
www.eurotool.com
• beading and jewelry-making tools

Fire Mountain Gems and Beads
800.355.2137 order line
800.423.2319 customer service
www.firemountaingems.com
• vast website and comprehensive catalog of beads, findings, tools, stringing materials and kits

Great Craft Works
888.811.5773
www.greatcraftworks.com
• beads, findings, tools, stringing materials

Global Curiosity Inc.
609.520.9881
• amazing handcrafted Russian beads

Houston Art Company
800.272.3804
www.houstonart.com
• craft products

Jacquard Products
Rupert, Gibbon and Spider, Inc.
800.442.0455
www.jacquardproducts.com
• inks, pigments, dyes, paints and artistic inspiration

JewelrySupply.Com
866.380.7464
www.jewelrysupply.com
• jewelry-making supplies: beads, findings, tools, stringing materials, packaging and display

J & O Fabrics
856.663.2121
www.jandofabrics.com
• fantastic fabrics

JudiKins
310.515.1115
www.judikins.com
• rubber stamps, Diamond Glaze

Kamibashi
828.683.7994
www.kamibashi.com
• fair trade Asian craft and textile imports

Making Memories
801.294.0430
www.makingmemories.com
• scrapbooking supplies

Marvin Schwab: The Bead
Warehouse
301.565.0487
www.thebeadwarehouse.com
• gems, jewelry, beads, findings and supplies

Match Feather
212.704.0111
• buttons, feathers and trim

Outside The Margins
209.236.1617
www.outsidethemargins.com
• bonanza of awesome retail scrapbook, card-making, jewelry and altered arts supplies

Paula Radke Dichroic Glass
805.772.5451
www.paularadke.com
• affordable and lovely dichroic glass beads

Phoenix Beads, Jewelry & Parts
and The Beads Depot, DIY
212.278.8688
www.phoenixbeads.com
www.thebeadsdepot.com
gemstone, glass, pearl and crystal beads from around the world

Plaid Enterprises, Inc.
800.842.4197
www.plaidonline.com
• craft supplies and
home décor products

Polyform Products
847.427.0020
www.sculpey.com
• polymer clay

Provo Craft
800.937.7686
www.provocraft.com
• scrapbook supplies and
general crafts

Prym Consumer USA Inc.
(formerly Prym Dritz)
www.dritz.com
• sewing notions and crafts

Rings & Things
800.366.2156
www.rings-things.com
• beads, tools, findings and
stringing materials

Riverstone Bead Company
219.939.2050
www.riverstonebead.com
• retail hand-polished and
drilled rock beads

Sacred Kitsch Studio
www.sacredkitschstudio.com
• funkadelic vintage and
retro ephemera, charms
and altered arts supplies

Simplicity
888.588.2700
www.simplicity.com
• sewing patterns

Swarovski North America
Limited
800.463.0849
www.create-your-style.com
• Swarovski crystal beads
and components

Thunderbird Supply
www.thunderbirdsupply.com
800.545.7968
• beads and precious metal findings

Tsukineko
800.769.6633
www.tsukineko.com
• pigments, dyes, craft ink products

Windsor and Newton
www.windsornewton.com
• fine art supplies

York Novelty
800.223.6676
212.594.7040
www.yorkbeads.com
• Czech glass beads

Wonder Sources Inc.
888.999.0478
www.wondersources.com
• premium and exotic
gemstone beads

sources

✛ **far away places necklace** page 24 crystal pearls from Swarovski; rice pearls and hematite beads from Fire Mountain Gems; metal spacers from Blue Moon Beads; clasp, connectors, findings and wire from Beadalon ✛ **muy caliente necklace** page 26 jasper pendant, sunstone, dzi, smoky quartz, carnelian and jade beads from Phoenix Jewelry and Parts; red jasper rondels from Thunderbird Supply; pewter clasp from The Bead Warehouse; wire, crimps and leather from Beadalon ✛ **break time badge holder** page 28 cereal box charms from Sacred Kitsch Studio; bead mix and metal rondels from Blue Moon Beads; jump rings and lobster clasp from Rings and Things; curved link chain from Eastern Findings ✛ **princess sparkle pants hip chain** page 30 chandelier component from Pure Allure; crystal beads and channel chain from Swarovski; lampwork teardrops and Czech glass beads from York Novelty; jump rings from Beadalon; lanyard clasps from Rings and Things ✛ **my end is my beginning bracelet** page 32 Russian tile bead from Global Curiosity; river stone beads from Riverstone Bead Company; vermeil beads from Fire Mountain Gems; findings from Beadalon ✛ **stone cold fox lariat** page 34 apple turquoise pendants from Wondersource; lime turquoise ovals from Fire Mountain Gems; turquoise heishi beads from Phoenix Jewelry and Parts; green pearls from Thunderbird Supply; Czech glass tiles from York Novelty; pewter tubes, jump rings and sterling chain from The Bead Warehouse; Hill Tribe Bee from Great Craft Works; wire guardians, crimp tubes and wire from Beadalon ✛ **aquatic garden necklace** page 36 hand-painted pendant from Global Curiosity; crystal beads from Swarovski; gunmetal eye pins from Rings and Things; Sparkle Podge from Plaid; Gum Arabic from Windsor and Newton; fabric markers from Fabrico ✛ **medusa necklace** page 40 Madness pendant from Global Curiosity; crystal pearls, channel chain and chandelier earrings from Swarovski; hematite beads from Phoenix Jewelry and Parts; Czech glass from York Novelty; filigree component and curb chain from Eastern Findings; honeycomb beads from Great Craft Works; findings and extension chain from Beadalon ✛ **cocky little purse charm** page 44 rooster bead from Phoenix Jewelry and Parts; Czech glass beads from York Novelty; porcelain beads from Global Curiosity; vermeil saucer from Fire Mountain Gems; findings and extension chain from Beadalon ✛ **how now, grazing cow choker** page 46 Swarovski crystal and pearls from Swarovski; sterling findings from The Bead Warehouse; memory wire and rubber tubing from Beadalon ✛ **sunrise special necklace** page 48 mother-of-pearl pendant from Phoenix Jewelry and Parts; yellow shell beads from Great Craft Works; brown rhodochrosite beads from The Bead Warehouse; miniature silverware charms from Blue Moon Beads; extension chain, jump rings, crimp clasp and wire from Beadalon ✛ **vamp choker** page 50 peacock feather fringe from Match Feather; frosted tube beads from Great Craft Works; filigrees from Swarovski; thread from Coats & Clark; grommet-setting tool and snaps from Prym Dritz ✛ **sea anemone bling ring** page 52 bling ring, ball-tip head pins and dichroic beads from Paula Radke; crystal teardrops from Swarovski; jade rice from Phoenix Jewelry and Parts; plain sterling head pins from The Bead Warehouse ✛ **five easy earrings** page 54 coral tubes, threader components and Etruscan bird clasp from Fire Mountain Gems; filigree flower components and chandelier components from Auntie's Beads; Czech glass from York Novelty; crystal beads from Swarovski; sterling jump rings, beads and head pins from The Bead Warehouse; jade lentils, carved flowers and jade ovals from Phoenix Jewelry and Parts; gold-plated wire and star-end head pins from Beadalon ✛ **"the ladies" purse** page 58 briolettes from Swarovski; bracelet blanks from Darice; findings from Beadalon; chicken feather trim from Match Feather; collage sheets from ARTchix Studio; thread from Coats & Clark; Diamond Glaze from Judikins

✛ **advertastic chandelier earrings** page 64 crystals from Swarovski; crystal chandelier components from Pure Allure; head pins and earwires from Beadalon ✛ **get well good luck charm bracelet** page 66 plastic gumball charms from Sacred Kitsch Studio; chain from Eastern Findings; heavy-duty jump rings from Rings and Things; clasp from Beadalon ✛ **enchanted tiara** page 68 crystal beads and pearls from Swarovski; metal headband from Goody; wire from Beadalon ✛ **pin-up boys purse** page 72 fabric from J and O Fabrics; bamboo handles from Match Feather; coral chips and pyrite from Phoenix Jewelry and Parts; lampwork beads from York Novelty; snaps and grommet setter from Prym Dritz; wire, crimps and clasps from Beadalon; pattern from Simplicity ✛ **domestic diva necklace** page 74 crystal beads from Swarovski; gunmetal head pins, eye pins and jump rings from Rings and Things; clasp from Beadalon ✛ **(you) go-go girl necklace** page 76 square channels from Swarovski; jump rings, extension chains and plated circles from Beadalon ✛ **under the microscope pin or pendant** page 78 microscope slides and copper tape from Outside the Margins; pin/pendant component from JewelrySupply.com; crystal chain from Swarovski; two-part epoxy from Beadalon ✛ **her story tank top** page 82 fabric transfer sheet from ARTchix Studio; beads from Elvee Rosenberg; Hot Fix crystals from Swarovski; fabric glue from Bond Adhesives ✛ **pms pendants** page 86 Page Pebbles from Memory Makers; Circle Pix from ARTchix Studio; findings from Beadalon; crystals from Swarovski; pendant blanks from Eastern Findings; Instant Grrrip craft cement from Bond Adhesives ✛ **monkey in the middle charm watch** 88 Tiger's eye, turquoise and bone beads from Phoenix Jewelry and Parts; sterling chain, head pins, clasp and beads from The Bead Warehouse; watch face from Pure Allure ✛ **pretty in pink watch** page 90 crystal beads and flowers, crystal earring component, clasp and watch face from Pure Allure; wire and head pins from Beadalon; Stop Fraying Glue from Aleene's ✛ **she walks in beauty pendant** page 92 crystals from Swarovski; circle pix images and optometrist's lens from ARTchix Studio; lock and key charm from Sacred Kitsch Studio; jump ring from Beadalon; Mod Podge from Plaid; Omni Gel from Houston Art, Inc. ✛ **my bonny lies over the ocean necklace** page 94 Czech glass beads from York Novelty; seed beads from Blue Moon Beads; glass ovals from Wondersource; Bali cones, eye pins, jump rings and clasps from The Bead Warehouse; wire from Beadalon ✛ **fly t-shirt** page 96 crystal beads and Hot Fix crystals from Swarovski; fabric transfer from ARTchix Studio; t-shirt from Old Navy; heavy-duty thread from Coats & Clark; Fabri-Tac adhesive from Beacon; fabric markers from Fabrico ✛ **auntie flo's pretty little tampon case** page 98 crystal beads from Swarovski; fabric transfer fairy from ARTchix Studio; felt from CPE; embroidery floss from DFN, Fabri-Tac adhesive from Beacon ✛ **nehalennia's net bracelet** page 104 metal mesh tubing from Elvee Rosenberg; dichroic beads from Paula Radke; crystal beads and pearls from Swarovski; findings from Beadalon ✛ **zombie boy key chain** page 106 Zombie String Gang™ Doll from Kamibashi; pearl cross from Phoenix Jewelry and Parts; crystal beads from Swarovski; patience medallion from Auntie's Beads; sterling key chain and findings from Fire Mountain Gems ✛ **scrappy chick charm pendant** page 108 scrapbook stickers from EK Success; scrapbook charms from Blue Moon Beads and Hirschberg Schutz; jump rings and clasps from Beadalon; crystal beads from Swarovski ✛ **pretty papers earrings** page 110 Page Pebbles from Memory Makers; handmade paper packs from Provo Craft; jump rings from Beadalon; sterling earwires from The Bead Warehouse ✛ **raku stretch bracelet** page 112 bracelet blanks by Darice; stamps by Rubber Stampede; Mod Podge by Plaid; StazOn ink by Tsukineko; Pearl Ex pigments by Jacquard Products; Elasticity by Beadalon; Hot Fix crystals by Swarovski ✛ **she's come unhinged bracelet** page 114 miniature dollhouse hinges from Craft-Inc.; GS Hypo Cement and all metal findings from Beadalon ✛ **crafty chick's bottle caps necklace and earrings** page 116 vintage bottle caps from Outside the Margins; metal chick charms from Sacred Kitsch Studio; crystal beads from Swarovski; chain and clasp from Beadalon; jump rings from Rings and Things; sterling earwires from The Bead Warehouse ✛ **p. ducky pendant** page 118 crystal beads from Swarovski; Premo!™ polymer clay from Polyform Products; eye pin from Rings and Things; Mod Podge from Plaid ✛ **day of the dead skull pin** page 120 crystal beads from Swarovski; pin finding from JewelrySupply.com; gunmetal findings from Rings and Things; Premo!™ polymer clay from Polyform Products; Sparkle Podge from Plaid

index

CHECK OUT THESE OTHER GREAT
NORTH LIGHT BOOKS
for inspiration and sassy crafting ideas!

The Impatient Beader

by Margot Potter

If you love to be creative and if you've caught the do-it-yourself bug but lack time, focus or motivation, *The Impatient Beader* is the book for you. In her debut book, author Margot Potter guides you through over 50 sassy jewelry projects, from the sweet—the Spunky Librarian Eyeglass Holder and the Dainty Debutante Bracelet—to the outright sizzling—the Disco Star Necklace and the Victorian Temptress Choker. You can finish each of the projects in just a few easy steps, and a skill level guide lets you know what you're getting into before you get going. An easy-to-follow techniques section shows you everything you need to get your bead on and cartoon Margot pops up every few pages to give you tips on how to become a beading goddess.

ISBN-13: 978-1-58180-762-2

ISBN-10: 1-58180-762-7 PAPERBACK, 128 PAGES, 33431

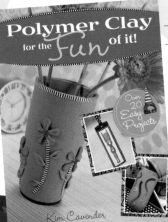

Simply Beautiful Beaded Jewelry

by Heidi Boyd

Author and designer Heidi Boyd has filled this fabulous jewelry book to the brim with over 50 gorgeous beaded necklaces, bracelets, earrings and accessories. Her trademark style shines in each of the projects and variations. Best of all, every piece is simple to make and beautiful to wear. Even a beginning crafter can easily finish any project in the book in one afternoon. The book includes a helpful techniques section and insightful tips scattered throughout.

ISBN-13: 978-1-58180-774-5

ISBN-10: 1-58180-774-0 PAPERBACK, 128 PAGES, 33445

Polymer Clay for the Fun of It!

by Kim Cavendar

With over 20 bright and colorful projects and variations, *Polymer Clay for the Fun of It!* shows readers how to have a good time with polymer clay. The book gives readers a comprehensive and light-hearted polymer clay "primer" along with a detailed techniques section to make getting started fun and easy. As a bonus feature, readers get "Just for the fun of it..." tips to keep them inspired. Each project begins with an often tongue-in-cheek quote that matches the easygoing tone of the book. With *Polymer Clay for the Fun of It!* you can throw all of the rules out the window and just, well, have fun!

ISBN-13: 978-1-58180-684-1

ISBN-10: 1-58180-684-7 PAPERBACK, 128 PAGES, 33320

Collage Discovery Workshop

by Claudine Hellmuth

This book is a medley of ideas, techniques and lessons on being an artist. Discover innovative techniques and demonstrations specifically designed to achieve the modern, eclectic collage effect that has become so popular today. Claudine Hellmuth will introduce you to the basics of collage, show you different image-transferring techniques and lead you through a series of creative exercises that are sure to ignite the creative spark in every crafter!

ISBN-13: 978-1-58180-343-3

ISBN-10: 1-58180-343-5 PAPERBACK, 128 PAGES, 32313

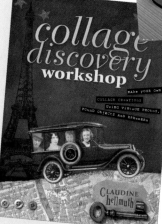

THESE AND OTHER FINE NORTH LIGHT TITLES ARE AVAILABLE FROM YOUR LOCAL ART AND CRAFT RETAILER, BOOKSTORE OR ONLINE SUPPLIER.